FROM TRIALS TO TRIUMPHS

Derek Prime

Regal Books

A Division of GL Publications
Ventura, CA U.S.A.

The translation of all Regal books is under the direction of
GLINT. GLINT provides technical help for the adaptation,
translation and publishing of books for millions of people
worldwide. For information regarding translation contact:
GLINT, P.O. Box 6688, Ventura, California 93006.

Second Printing, 1983

Published by Regal Books
A Division of GL Publications
Ventura, California 93006
Printed in U.S.A.

Library of Congress Cataloging in Publication Data
Prime, Derek.
    From trials to triumphs.

    (Bible commentary for laymen)
    1. Bible. N.T. James—Commentaries.   I. Title.
II. Series
BS2785.3.P74   1982   227'.91077   82-13351
ISBN 0-8307-0821-9

CONTENTS

A Teacher's Manual and Student Discovery Guide for Bible study groups using this course are available from your church supplier.

One

MEET THE WRITER AND HIS READERS!
James 1:1

James, a servant of God and of the Lord Jesus Christ, to the twelve tribes scattered among the nations: Greetings.

To know something of a writer's identity and his original readers' circumstances always helps us to understand better what he writes. But we immediately face something of a problem here!

Which James?

Five people are called James in the New Testament. The name itself is the Greek equivalent of the Jewish name *Jacob*. Let's say, first of all, *who it is not*.

The James who writes this letter isn't James the son of Zebedee, the Galilean fisherman, brother of John, and member of the Twelve, who was executed by Herod Agrippa (Acts 12:2).

Neither is he James the son of Alphaeus, who also belonged to the Twelve (Matt. 10:3); nor is he James the son of Mary (Matt. 27:56), called James the small or the younger (Mark 15:40). (It is possible that James the son of Alphaeus and James the son of Mary are one and the same person.) And, finally, he isn't James the father of an apostle named Judas, mentioned only by Luke (6:16; Acts 1:13).

We are left with James, the Lord's brother (Matt. 13:55; Mark 6:3) who was prominent in the leadership of the church at Jerusalem (Acts 15:13; 21:18). The respect the early Christians had for his leadership explains why they looked to him for guidance as he wrote to them under the Holy Spirit's direction.

Jews or Gentiles?

Having identified the writer, we now have the task of establishing the identity of his readers—a subject of controversy over the years. James refers to "the twelve tribes scattered among the nations," and in so doing he uses a technical term "the dispersion." John 7:35 also uses the word *dispersion* ("scattered" in *NIV*) to refer to the scattered Jews living outside Palestine. This reference has led many to suppose that James—who was himself a Jew, of course—has only Jewish Christians in view as he writes.

But that is an opinion of only some, and it seems to make much better sense to think of James's letter as having been written to *both* Jews and Gentiles. Nowhere does James provide any other possible clues that he may have solely Jewish Christians in mind. It is a New Testament principle that in Christ "there is no Greek or Jew, circumcised or uncircumcised" (Col. 3:11), and it was James himself who, in what we know as "the Council at Jerusalem," took important initiative to maintain the unity of God's people (Acts 15:19). Furthermore, there is no instruction in James's letter which has a particular Jewish reference. Rather its instruction is relevant to all Christians—then as now.

What seems to tip the balances finally, in confirmation of this view, is that the apostle Peter uses an almost identical description of his readers (1 Peter 1:1), and his language elsewhere in his first letter makes it plain that he has Gentiles as well as Jews in mind (2:9,10).

James's Self-Description

James could have introduced himself as "James, the brother of Jesus Christ," but he doesn't. The way in which we introduce ourselves to others, as well as the way we like others to introduce us, says quite a lot about us. James's self-description indicates the virtue of humility on his part and his understanding that a spiritual relationship to Jesus Christ is the most important thing (see 2 Cor. 5:16), and every Christian, by the grace of God, possesses that amazing boon.

Instead, James introduces himself as "*a servant of God and of the Lord Jesus Christ.*" He copies the apostles in this self-description, for they all recognized themselves to be unconditionally obliged to serve God's people (2 Cor. 4:5). Both Paul (Rom. 1:1; Titus 1:1) and Peter (2 Pet. 1:1) begin their letters in a similar way.

Literally, the word *servant* can be translated "slave." James was completely committed to the service of God and of His Son Jesus Christ. This commitment was a voluntary commitment which makes the use of the word *servant* or *slave* all the more meaningful. Service was James's delight. He could have identified with the sense of dignity which surrounds Paul's words to the Colossians, some of whom were slaves, "It is the Lord Christ you are serving" (Col. 3:24).

I remember visiting an elderly lady who had spent all her working life as a nanny for aristocratic English families. She had been "in service" for them. But the significant memory I have is that there was nothing "servile" about her. She spoke with glowing pride of her employers and the children they had committed to her care. She was proud of being "a servant" on at least two accounts: first, she knew the importance of those whom she served, and she unashamedly respected them; and, second, she was treated by her employers with such love and kindness that she was never made to feel a "servant" but rather a valued member of the family.

There's no greater dignity than that of a servant of the Lord Christ, the King of kings. Serving Him, we both please and serve God the Father who sent His Son into the world. But there is nothing servile about our service of God and His Son. God treats us with amazing kindness, and actually adopts us into His family. While we rightly call ourselves "servants," He, nevertheless, calls us "sons," "daughters," and "friends" (John 15:15).

The term "servant" is a favorite description of the Christian because Jesus Christ, our heavenly Lord, appeared on earth in the form of a servant (Phil. 2:7), and we are never more like our Lord Jesus than when we serve God by becoming the willing servants of others, for Jesus' sake, with no limits set (2 Cor. 4:5). One of the most memorable incidents in the Gospels—Jesus' washing of the disciples' feet—was intended to teach this lesson (John 13:1-17, and especially verses 14-16).

The Servant's Master

James doesn't introduce himself simply as "a servant of Jesus" or "a servant of Christ" but he uses a much fuller description of the Son of God, whose earthly brother he had been. James was "a servant of God and of *the Lord Jesus Christ.*"

The use of the word *Lord* in the first century immediately raised Jesus above the human level. James had not found it easy to recognize that the

One he knew as his older brother was, in fact, God Incarnate; and, together with the other members of the family of Joseph and Mary, he failed to believe in Him at first. But as understanding dawned, so commitment to the Lord Jesus began.

James had used the title *Lord* long before he knew Jesus to be God. It is the word employed in the Greek translation of the Old Testament to render the name of God, "Jehovah." It is used regularly of Christ in the New Testament, meaning that He is the divine Lord, having the highest place of all, worthy of our worship, service and obedience (Acts 2:36; 1 Cor. 16:22; Phil. 2:9-11; Col. 3:24).

Jesus is the Greek form of the Hebrew name *Joshua*, meaning "God is salvation" or "God is the Saviour." In obedience to God's command, it was given to the Son of God when He became man, a symbol of God's promise that Christ would rescue God's people from the guilt and power of their sins (Matt. 1:21; Luke 1:31; 2:21).

Christ is a Greek word signifying "the Anointed One"—the meaning of the word *Messiah*. Anointing was a symbol of being set apart for a special task by God. The Jews looked for the coming of a Great One, called the Messiah, who would accomplish God's purposes for His people. The Lord Jesus accepted the title, but only infrequently, for it would appear that the Jews mainly thought of the Messiah as a political deliverer and Jesus had not come as such (Matt. 16:16,17; Mark 14:61,62; John 4:25,26; see also Matt. 1:18; 2:4; Luke 2:11,26).

James's description of our Lord Jesus Christ is really his testimony. As a member of a family circle from the time of his birth he had known his brother Jesus—the man—and he had appreciated the meaning of His name. Eventually, through the teaching and miracles of Jesus, and in particular His resurrection, James had come to see that Jesus was not only the promised Messiah but also the Son of God who was the Lamb of God, the One who bears away not only the sins of Jews who believe but the sins of *all* who believe.

A Key Description of Christians

Christians—whether Jews or Gentiles—are God's scattered people. The New Testament goes to great pains to show that Christians—whether Jews or Gentiles—are God's true and spiritual Israel (see 1 Pet. 2:9,10). It takes pleasure, therefore, in using Old Testament pictures to illustrate New Testament truths.

When the Jewish people were described as "the dispersion," it was a reminder that wherever they might be scattered their real home was Palestine, and that their loyalty to Palestine was superior to all other loyalties. Alive in every Jew scattered among the nations was the hope of one day going to his true home in Palestine, and in particular to Jerusalem.

Christians today are scattered among the nations. There are many differences between them and they bear different names—even as the twelve Jewish tribes did; but they are one people, though scattered and speaking many languages. Wherever they live, and no matter how rightly loyal they are as good citizens of the nations in which God has placed them, they know that their true home is heaven (Phil. 3:20), and that they must live in this world "as aliens and strangers" (1 Pet. 2:11).

Great and glorious moments have occurred in Jewish history when members of the dispersed nation have been called back to their true home. The great hope of all true Christians, scattered among the tribes and nations of the world, is the return of the Son of God with power and great glory when "he will send his angels with a loud trumpet call, and they will gather his elect from the four winds, from one end of the heavens to the other" (Matt. 24:31).

Meanwhile, Christians rejoice to know of one another's existence and to recognize and greet one another. (Notice James's word *greetings*.) They recognize too their duty to live in such a way that they display their heavenly citizenship in everyday life and are ready for the return of their Master. It is about this duty that James now writes.

To serve others for Jesus' sake, we need to have the same attitude as He displayed (Phil. 2:5). What does that mean in practice?

To remember that we are part of the Christian "dispersion" is to remember that our true citizenship is in heaven (Phil 3:20). How should this affect our life-style?

How do we put into contemporary terms the concepts of our being "aliens" and "strangers" (1 Pet. 2:11)?

Two

FACING TRIALS
James 1:2-8

To live successfully in the world we must know how to face up to trials. James writes on this subject because he appreciates that his readers are going through difficult experiences that they would never have chosen for themselves. He wants to be a good pastor to them. Therefore he must be sympathetic yet honest, and sometimes blunt.

Developing Right Attitudes

Attitudes are all-important. "Consider it pure joy . . ." (Jas. 1:2). The kind of people we are and the behavior we adopt are all determined by the inner attitudes we develop. Our prevailing attitudes to life color our whole personality and experience of life (Prov. 15:13,15). God's concern is that our attitudes should be right (Phil. 2:5) for then our actions, for the most part, will take care of themselves (see Phil. 2:1-4).

To arrive at correct conduct, therefore, we have to be honest and begin with our mind, with the way we think. Part of our essential experience of salvation is the renewal of our mind so that we may be able to test and approve what God's will is (Rom. 12:2).

By his use of the word "consider" in verse 2, James emphasizes that there are things we have to look at deliberately in a particular way if we are to arrive at the right conclusions, and this is certainly the case when it comes to trials.

Attitudes are determined by understanding. In verse 3 he writes of something that his readers "know." It is the things that we are sure of which influence our reactions as difficult circumstances or crises arise in our lives.

To be well taught in the Scriptures is strategically important because one of the principal purposes of Christian instruction is to provide a foundation of knowledge upon which we can build our lives through the development of proper attitudes. For example, trouble, hardship and various forms of suffering come to all of us at some time or another. The natural tendency may be to feel that such things are a waste of human life and to be avoided at all costs. But not at all! Knowledge informs us otherwise. "We *know* that in all things God works for the good of those who love him, who have been called according to his purpose" (Rom. 8:28).

Facing Trials

There are truths God has revealed about trials which are intended to influence and determine our attitudes. (We ought to notice in passing that the word "trial" in James 1:2 can also be translated "temptation." It is used in the good sense of God or our Lord Jesus Christ putting us to the test so that we may prove ourselves true, and then in the bad sense—and never of God—enticement to sin. At this point in James's letter it is right to translate it "trials.")

Trials are inevitable. Trials are an expected feature of ordinary human life and also of the Christian life. James takes that fact for granted. He does not write "*if* you face trials" but "*whenever* you face trials." To escape trials we would have to escape from this world altogether.

Trials are various in nature. We have to face trials of "many kinds." Some trials come according to the age of life we have attained. Young people, for example, know the trials which accompany their development into adulthood and the tests which come through having to learn to keep under control their natural desires and bodily appetites.

Older people are not exempt from these same trials since the battle against sin does not grow easier as we grow older. Furthermore, trials come with old age, when things we used to be able to do we can do no longer.

Seemingly unique trials come also with the various responsibilities of life. Parenthood, for example, is glorious and exciting in prospect, but in reality it brings its own trials if children are wayward and do not respond readily to discipline.

Job promotion is a tremendous encouragement, but the responsibilities it brings may be overwhelming.

Trials are *multi-colored*—that's the word James uses—and they are as diverse as the colors of the rainbow and all the permutations of shades of color which are possible. The lovely thing to remember, however, is that just as the trials that come to us are many-colored so too is God's grace (1 Peter 4:10).

Trials tend to come upon us unexpectedly. The verb "face" is really the verb "fall into." It is the verb used of the traveler who *fell into* the hands of robbers in the story of the Good Samaritan (Luke 10:30), and of the ship carrying the apostle Paul that "*struck* a sandbar and ran aground" (Acts 27:41). Both uses imply the unexpected nature of the events.

Trials may be around the next corner. We can seldom anticipate them, which may of course be just as well. At any moment we may meet an old difficulty or a new one. The unexpected nature of trials makes it all the more necessary that we should be prepared beforehand with the knowledge of how to react to them.

Trials test faith. The word *faith* occurs often without an object, as here in James 1:3, signifying true piety or genuine religion. It means simply *being a Christian* because being a Christian is all about having faith in God through His Son Jesus Christ. James could equally well have written, "because you know that the testing of you *as a Christian* develops perseverance."

But besides being a term which sums up what it means to be a Christian, faith is also a Christian virtue (1 Thess. 3:6). Faith is essentially our response to God's faithfulness. It begins as our response to God in the glorious revelation He has given of Himself in our Lord Jesus Christ. The Lord Jesus Christ Himself is the originator of our faith ("author," Heb. 12:2) because it is as we realize His complete trustworthiness and the perfection of all that He has done on our behalf as our Saviour that we exercise faith in Him and the promises He makes to us in the Gospel.

Faith is intended to grow. The One in whom we trust is greater than we can ever imagine, and no matter how great our faith grows, it can never outmatch the greatness of God as He has revealed Himself in the Lord Jesus.

Trials test faith both from the point of view of proving its genuineness and from the point of view of making it grow. Faith is not simply a matter of *words*, it is also a matter of *deeds*. Trials put faith in the refining fire, and pure faith always emerges out of the furnace brighter and stronger. Samuel Rutherford (1600-1661), whose letters from prison are a spiritual treasury, wrote, "Praise God for the hammer, the file, and the furnace." The word for testing is used elsewhere for the testing of metals to prove their genuineness. Even as currency is of use only as it is genuine and stands up to the tests men may use to prove its genuineness, so our lives have usefulness to God in the world only as faith is proved to be true faith.

Trials develop perseverance (Jas. 1:3). Perseverance is an important Christian virtue. It is another word for patience, endurance, fortitude or steadfastness. It is the ability to hold on, and to see a situation through to its proper conclusion. It is "stickability" at its best.

An important characteristic of true faith is that it does not collapse when tested. Rather, like the muscles in my arm, it grows through exercise. God knows exactly how much we can take at any time of testing, and He sees to it that our trials are never beyond the power of our faith, at the stage it is, to respond (1 Cor. 10:13).

We need to be clear as to the practical application of this perseverance. When trials come we tend to feel that there is little point in continuing in the good things we know we ought to do because, on the apparent and deceptive evidence of our trials, we are not being rewarded for the good we do. That's the kind of whispered insinuation we may expect from Satan, the great enemy of our souls. But genuine faith perseveres in doing good, whatever the circumstances. As lifeboat men go out to do what they can for people in distress irrespective of the weather, so faith goes on doing the right thing whatever the moral and spiritual climate.

Physical suffering may become so acute at times that we can scarcely help ourselves, being preoccupied with our own needs. When physical hardship occurs on account of our loyalty to Christ, we may be tempted to feel that it is a large price to pay. But genuine faith still perseveres and endures the suffering gladly for Christ's sake (see Acts 5:40,41).

Obedience to Christ, especially with regard to the service in which He calls us to engage in His name, may bring innumerable hardships (see 2 Cor. 6:4-10). Faith holds on, nevertheless, counting it a privilege to serve such a Master (2 Tim. 2:10).

Arthur Matthews, a missionary in China, wrote home sharing some of the difficulties he and his family were enduring: "These trials of faith are to give us patience, for patience can only be worked as faith goes into the Pressure Chamber. To pull out because the pressure is laid on, and to start fretting would be to lose all the good He has in it for us."

Trials need to be responded to properly. "Perseverance must finish its work" (Jas. 1:4). One of the dangers of trials, either when they actually happen or as we see them appear on the horizon of our life, is our tendency to try to escape them in some way or another, or to endeavor to avoid their full force rather than to see them through to God's planned conclusion. We must deliberately let endurance show itself in practice. We must prove to ourselves—as well as to the silent spectators who may be watching to see how real our faith is when it is tested—that perseverance is both possible and profitable.

Isobel Kuhn, in her book, *Green Leaf in Drought Time*, describes how some missionary friends found great encouragement in Andrew Murray's formula for trial.

"1. Say, He brought me here. It is by His will I am in this strait place and in that fact I will rest.

"2. He will keep me here in His love and give me grace to behave as His child.

"3. Then He will make the trial a blessing, teaching me the lessons He intends for me to learn.

"4. In His good time He can bring me out again—how and when He knows. So let me say, I am (1) here by God's appointment; (2) in His keeping; (3) under His training; (4) for His time."[1]

Trials, properly responded to, are always fruitful. Perseverance must be allowed to complete its work so that we "may be mature and complete, not lacking anything" (1:4).

Three aspects of the fruitfulness of trials are mentioned. First, they make us *mature.* Maturity is spiritual adulthood; it is our attaining the purposes and ends God has for our life. It is not we who determine what maturity is, but God; and it is God who also chooses the means by which we arrive at maturity—that is to say, trials! Maturity is hopelessly hindered if we try to escape God's purposes in the testings He either permits or sends. We remain spiritual children rather than becoming spiritual adults, and we are then unable to be spiritually useful in the care of new spiritual babes.

Second, trials make us *complete.* God the Holy Spirit always has a particular goal in view, whatever life may be doing to us, and that goal is Christlikeness. Christlikeness is the completeness at which the Holy Spirit aims in our sanctification. The goal, therefore, of our various testings is that we should become more and more like our Saviour. The whole of Christ's character is to be reproduced in us, and this is possible only as we respond willingly and submissively to God's purposes in our trials.

Third, trials bring us to the position where we are *not lacking in anything.* This expression simply conveys the thought of maturity and completeness in a negative manner. As trials are allowed to do their proper work of leading us on to maturity and completeness, so we are in the happy position of not lacking any good benefit God intends us to possess.

The message James would have us grasp is that

solid achievement in the Christian life usually comes about only through the testing of our faith. When God is at work in us He first inspires faith, and He then perfects that faith (Heb. 12:2). Its maturity is one of His major concerns. To appreciate this basic fact makes sense of many of the unpleasant experiences God permits.

Charles Simeon of Cambridge, whose ministry exercised such a tremendous influence at the end of the seventeenth and the beginning of the eighteenth centuries in England, went through some months of dreadful strain and humiliation. In a letter to a very close friend, he wrote, "They who are most earnest in prayer for grace, are often most afflicted, because the graces which they pray for, e.g. faith, hope, patience, humility etc. are only to be wrought in us by means of those trials which call forth the several graces into act and exercise."

Trials, therefore, properly understood, occasion joy. We are now in a position to appreciate James's opening words: *"Consider it pure joy,* my brothers, whenever you face trials of many kinds" (1:2). We are able to *consider* trials as a source of joy. It would be a sign of a disordered mind to equate trials for their own sakes as a source of joy! But they may be *considered* as a proper ground for joy when we recognize the fruit that God intends shall flow from them. Perhaps the most important lesson we must learn from what James says is that the benefit we receive from trials depends to a large degree upon how we look at them and the spirit with which we handle them.

When we see trials as a privilege our heavenly Father allows because He wants His Spirit to perfect His work of making us like our Lord Jesus—to make us "complete" Christians—we discover a joy in our trials, a joy the Holy Spirit gives (Rom. 14:17). Faith itself gives and knows its own particular joy (Phil. 1:25; 1 Pet. 1:8) and it is our faith that is perfected and increased as we submit to God's purposes in times of testing.

Obtaining Wisdom

But to be honest and realistic, it is not always easy to adopt this right attitude, much as we want to do so, both beforehand and as and when trials arise. We lack the wisdom so often to know how to handle the difficulties which come in the course of daily life. The reason we have sometimes made a mess of our handling of trials, so that they have not produced spiritual fruit, is that we have lacked wisdom.

The glorious truth is, however, that we have a heavenly Father who delights to give wisdom to His children. The wisdom Solomon knew, a wisdom that astounded his contemporaries, was bestowed upon him as a result of his request to God (1 Kings 3:9). The reason Stephen's opponents could not stand up against his wisdom was because he was filled with God's Spirit (Acts 6:5,10). The remarkable wisdom Paul displays in his New Testament letters was the consequence of "the wisdom that God gave him" (2 Pet. 3:15).

It is, however, a wisdom for which we must ask (Jas. 1:5). There is a basic and simple principle here: we must ask in order to receive—that is how God has purposely ordered things. We do not have to apologize that we tend to think of prayer as principally a matter of asking God for various benefits. If we examine all the Bible references to prayer, the great majority imply that prayer *is* essentially *asking* God for things. It is of course much more, and prayer is, not least, communion with God.

But our heavenly Father, like all good fathers, delights to meet His children's needs and rejoices in the proper dependence we show upon Him as we come only to Him for some of our foremost necessities. Since He is the source of all wisdom—He is the only wise God (Rom. 16:27)—it is no surprise that the wisdom we require to respond properly to our trials is given in answer to prayer to our Father.

We must ask believingly for wisdom. We "must believe and not doubt" (Jas 1:6). Acceptable prayer is based on faith, not doubt. Prayer must be our *first* recourse, not our second or last. Believing prayer has as its basis the confidence that God "exists and that he rewards those who earnestly seek him" (Heb. 11:6). Faith enables us to ask God for what He promises, and we are never disappointed.

Not to ask believingly is disastrous. Although the context is quite different, the principle Paul expounded to the Romans applies here also: "Everything that does not come from faith is sin" (Rom. 14:23). To pray and, at the same time, not to believe that God either hears or will answer is an offence against God—a dreadful sin. The doubter is a man who prays but then goes out and acts as if he has not prayed. His professed beliefs do not coincide with his actions. He tries to ride two horses at once—faith and doubt—and he is at odds with himself.

Now we may all find ourselves troubled by doubts from time to time, and few of us escape them. But the thing to do with our doubts is to bring them out into the open in our fellowship with God. We may ask God for wisdom to solve our doubts. The answer to most of them is to consider the revealed character of God, to see and to ponder God's glory in the face of our Lord Jesus Christ (2 Cor. 4:6).

The man, however, who refuses to be honest with both himself and God about his doubts condemns himself by his own behavior. He becomes as unstable as the waves of the sea, tossed and blown by the wind (Jas. 1:6,8; James delights to use illustrations from nature, and this is his first).

The tragedy of the doubter—or the double-minded man—is that he receives nothing from God (1:7). His behavior does not fit in with the behavior of the God to whom he thinks he comes in prayer. God never wavers or fluctuates (1:17), and He requires that those who come to Him should aim at being the same.

We must ask in prayer, therefore, without double-mindedness. In the particular context of what James writes here, that means that we must ask God for wisdom with the specific purpose and honest intention of responding to our trials in such a way that all of God's purposes in them are fulfilled.

It will not do, for example, to ask for wisdom, and then, when we receive it from God, decide that we prefer to do things our own way. That is a plain form of double-mindedness. If we really trust God, we recognize that His way is best before we even know what it is. If we ask Him for wisdom with this confidence we shall not lack it. Rather we shall receive it in abundance. God will give us generously the wisdom we need (1:5). There is nothing mean or niggardly about God's giving. And so it is that when we receive God's wisdom, we *know* that we have it, and we move forward with certainty and without hesitancy.

Not only will God give us wisdom generously, but He will also give it "without finding fault" (1:5). We ourselves may have fallen into the snare of giving help to someone but providing it in such a way that we are saying, in effect, "You ought not to have come to me for help again. What an undeserving person you are!" God does not deal with us like that. He is glad for us to come to Him as often as we are willing to come. And the more we come, the more He pours out His wisdom upon us, so that even when the most difficult trials occur we are able to "consider it pure joy" because we know He will provide us with the wisdom to enable us to cooperate with Him in them. The wisdom He imparts ensures that we gain the maximum benefit from them, and that His purposes of maturity and completeness in our life move on to further important stages.

If we need to begin with our mind in order to have a right attitude towards trials and temptations, what are the priorities for our mind? (See, for example, Romans 12:1,2; Phil. 2:5; 4:8 and 1 Pet. 1:13.)

Which Bible characters stand out as men and women who were subjected to particular testing? In what ways did they show perseverance? What were the fruits of their trials?

If a Christian says, "I think I ought to change my job because my place of employment is not an easy place to work," how would you counsel him in the light of what James teaches?

Note

1. Isobel S. Kuhn, *Green Leaf in Drought Time* (Chicago: Moody Press, 1957).

Three

RIGHT PERSPECTIVES
James 1:9-18

Perspectives for living are vital. The way in which we think about life in general determines the manner in which we react to the challenges and pressures of life. To have a right perspective on life is to see everything in its proper place and to come to a right judgment which, in turn, will bring about right behavior.

James's plea to "consider it pure joy, my brothers, whenever you face trials of many kinds" (1:2), is a plea for correct perspectives in Christian living. Our perspective upon life depends upon our application of spiritual truth. James now urges that we should have Christian perspectives on poverty and wealth on the one hand, and trials and temptations on the other.

Poverty and Wealth

Poverty was as great a problem in first-century society (Jas. 1:9-11) as it is in many parts of the world today. People tended either to be very rich or very poor, with the rich always getting richer and the poor poorer. The wealthy man in the New Testament was usually the man who did not need to work for his living (Matt. 27:57; Luke 12:16; see also Luke 16:1,19; 18:23; 19:2).

Poverty is a trial. It may make a person ashamed and take away his dignity. It is a particular testing for the breadwinner in the family because he may feel a sense of failure which cripples his self-respect.

The Christian, however, if he is guided by the instruction of God's Word, has a new perspective upon poverty and wealth. *First, he now knows what real riches are.* Once he may have thought that wealth consisted of savings in the bank, a luxurious home, and all the things money can buy. But he now knows that real wealth is both spiritual and eternal, the riches Jesus Christ gives to those who trust Him. To be born again into God's family is to have our eyes opened to the fact that the visible wealth of this world is not real wealth at all.

James uses nature often in order to illustrate spiritual truth, for what is true in nature is frequently paralleled in the spiritual realm. The wealthy are like the blossom of a wild flower which quickly passes away (1:10,11). The wealthy person may think that his life is all planned and certain. He may carefully arrange his business trips and calculate the new profit he intends to make. But in fact his life may be taken from him "while he goes about his business" (1:11). Man tends to assume he has plenty of time in the future. But just as he does not know the time that the withered blossom of a flower will fall, so he does not know the moment God will bring his life to an end. As he sits in the stock exchange or chairs a board meeting, God may suddenly call him to account.

Second, the Christian knows something of what his real wealth is in Jesus Christ. At the heart of the good news is the revelation that our Lord Jesus

Christ became poor for our sakes, so that we through His poverty might be rich (2 Cor. 8:9). God "has blessed us in the heavenly realms with every spiritual blessing in Christ" (Eph. 1:3). "No eye has seen, no ear has heard, no mind has conceived what God has prepared for those who love him" (1 Cor 2:9; see also Isa. 64:4). When John Newton knew failure in money matters at one stage in his life, he expressed his thoughts to his wife: "We want for nothing at present . . . perhaps we may not be rich . . . no matter . . . We are rich indeed if the promises and providence of God are our inheritance."

There are, happily, things which will never pass away (Matt. 5:18; 24:35; Mark 13:31), and among these are the words and promises of God. "Treasures in heaven" are beyond the reach of all fluctuation and decay and will prove no disappointment but rather an eternal and exciting surprise (Matt. 6:20). Having treasure in heaven is like having a purse that does not wear out (Luke 12:33).

Third, the Christian knows the difference that the Lord's coming is going to make to the world's values. The man who puts his confidence in wealth is like a plant without good roots (compare Matt. 13:6; Mark 4:6). The resources of the wealthy will lose all value at the judgment, and nothing they have stored up will have any validity in the life to come. On the other hand, the Christian poor will discover things to be very different. The poor find that their poverty frequently brings humiliation; but the judgment will reverse that situation. So often the poor are unable to obtain justice; but the judgment will reverse that position too.

The Christian in humble circumstances, therefore, may take legitimate pride in his high position in Christ (Jas. 1:9), and he *will* do so *if his perspective is right.* Whatever his poverty, he is the object of his Almighty Father's care, and he is one for whom the

Son of God, the Lord of glory, shed His blood. He may be legitimately proud of what God does for a man when no one else cares very much about him (1 Cor. 1:26-31). He has proved that God comforts the downhearted (Isa. 49:13; 2 Cor. 7:6). The remarkable paradox is that in the light of these truths he may live his life with a greater dignity and joy than does the wealthy man who puts his trust in wealth rather than in God through Jesus Christ. It is an established fact of history that Christianity has given new hope and dignity to people whose circumstances, to say the least, have been humble and sometimes almost unbearable.

On the other hand, the Christian whose circumstances are the opposite—in that he is wealthy and affluent—should remember how ephemeral these circumstances are. James may be using irony in verse 10 if he has in mind wealthy people who are not Christians, for they are most unlikely to take his advice! But the Christian who has material wealth needs to heed James's advice too. There is nothing wrong in possessing wealth; the wrong, if wrong there be, is in the misuse of it, and any wrongful attitude toward it (1 Tim. 6:17-19). Overvalued possessions tend to possess their owners. The person who has wealth needs to appreciate that the God who has made it possible for him to be affluent also makes him accountable; the sun which makes the flower grow also has the power to make it wither (Jas. 1:11).

Materially wealthy Christians should cultivate a proper attitude to their material possessions and take pride in the understanding God gives them concerning them. They will then use them all the more wisely and "lay up treasure for themselves as a firm foundation for the coming age" (1 Tim. 6:19). Over all material wealth we ought to write, "Perishing," because both we ourselves and our worldly possessions are due to fade away.

When we possess a right perspective on poverty and wealth we come to appreciate that wealth may be a greater trial—although a hidden one—than poverty! Many have found that their wealth has made them neglect their souls' welfare.

Trials and Temptations

Trials have already been James's subject in verses 2-4. The instruction he provides concerning wisdom (1:5-8) also has trials as its context. And, as we have just seen, his discussion of poverty is on account of the obvious trial it was to many of his first-century readers. He returns to the topic more specifically in verses 12-18: "Blessed is the man who perseveres under trial, because when he has stood the test, he will receive the [victor's] crown of life that God has promised to those who love him" (1:12).

James underlines *the worthwhileness of persevering under trial*. Trials, whether of poverty, social injustice, illness, or of any sort, are not easy to put up with at any time. But the first priority for the Christian in the face of any trial is *perseverance*. And that perseverance, as we have seen, must be allowed to finish its work if the trial is to yield the fruit of spiritual maturity (1:4).

We have noted already that the same Greek word can be translated both "trial" and "temptation," and James may have both in view here. As Thomas Brooks (1608-1680) wrote, "Times of affliction often prove times of great temptations, and therefore afflictions are called temptations." Trials and temptations, however, require different sorts of perseverance.

To persevere in a trial is to see it through to its completion. To persevere in a trial is to remain instead of fleeing, to stand one's ground and to hold on no matter how difficult it may be to do so. Perseverance in trials involves the determination to refuse to run away from difficulties so as to ensure that God's purposes in and through the trials are not missed but discovered and enjoyed.

To persevere in temptation, however, is to hold on to what is right and to persevere in resisting the temptation until such a time as the temptation is either removed or loses its power. Sometimes, of course, trials and temptations cannot be disentangled since Satan schemes to make our trials—which God permits—to become also a source of temptation to us as Satan encourages us to doubt God's goodness and love in allowing such trials.

Perseverance is worthwhile because, first of all, we prove our faith—our Christian profession—to be genuine by means of it. True faith, when it is under trial, stands "the test" (1:12). This was the precise emphasis of our Lord Jesus Himself in the parable of the sower; "Those on the rock are the ones who receive the word with joy when they hear it, but they have no root. They believe for a while, but in the time of testing they fall away" (Luke 8:13). There are trials that God *permits* (as in the case of Job, to be referred to later by James in 5:11), and there are also trials that God *sends*. He puts men to the test that they may prove themselves, and the outcome is always for the best (John 6:6; Heb. 11:17; Gen. 22:1). Peter has an emphasis similar to James's for, writing of trials, he declares, "These have come so that your faith—of greater worth than gold, which perishes even though refined by fire—may be proved genuine and may result in praise, glory and honor when Jesus Christ is revealed" (1 Pet. 1:7).

Second, perseverance is worthwhile because we shall reap its rewards in the life to come. "The [victor's] crown" (1:12) is a picture of eternal life, and eternal life is the great hope God sets before His people. He promises it to us, and He is the God who cannot lie (Titus 1:2). The fact that God gives this vic-

tor's crown "to those who love him" must not lead us
to think of eternal life as something that we earn. We
know only too well that we love God because He has
first loved us (1 John 4:19). But loving God—in
response to our discovery of His amazing love to us in
Jesus Christ—we respond with perseverance and
faithfulness in "the race marked out for us" (Heb.
12:1), and God delights to reward faithful believers.

A very practical example of faithfulness to God is
our perseverance in obedience to Him when He allows
trials to come, and when we persevere in doing right
when temptation confronts us. When we appreciate
the place of trials and temptations in proving the
genuineness of our faith, and we see how they feed
our expectation of what is ours in the life to come, we
find ourselves discovering joy in the whole process,
uncomfortable as the process itself may be. We really
"consider it pure joy."

Real wealth, following on from what we have discovered from James 1:9-11, is not the transitory
wealth which comes from this world's commerce, but
the spiritual and eternal wealth which comes from
being approved by God as His children through testing. Properly understood, therefore, trials and temptations are grounds for happiness. By our proper
attitude to them we establish our identity as God's
children. By our overcoming of them we confirm our
assurance of everlasting life. We may count ourselves
"blessed" when we persevere under trial.

The Source of Temptation

When we think of temptation, in distinction from
trials, we need to appreciate *the importance of recognizing the principal source of temptation.* While it is
true that God gives blessing and encouragement to
those who are tested and tempted, it is important to
recognize that God has no hand in actually tempting
us. God is never the source of our temptations (Jas.

1:13). Temptation may be summed up as enticement to sin and to evil (Gal. 6:1). God cannot be tempted by evil, and He does not tempt anyone.

Temptations begin with our own individual desires, and many of those desires may be evil (Jas. 1:14). Evil may be defined as anything that is contrary to God's law and will. Our soul falls victim to evil, contrary often to its own efforts and in spite of its struggles (see Rom. 7:18-21). It would be quite wrong, of course, to suggest that all of our desires are evil. The word *desire* can be used in a good sense (Prov. 10:24; Luke 22:15; Phil. 1:23) as well as bad. But all our desires, as a consequence of the fall, have an unhappy potential for evil.

Sometimes the cravings of our flesh (Gal. 5:16) may be uppermost in our desires. Satan, the great enemy of our souls, knows how to make the most of our evil desires. He is called "the tempter" (Matt. 4:3; 1 Thess. 3:5) because one of his principal activities is to tempt men and women (1 Cor. 7:5; Rev. 2:10).

There is no period in the Christian life when we are exempt from temptation. Those we experience early on in the Christian life may well be different from those we experience later, but the spiritual battle continues until the end.

Usually Satan's procedure is to lay bait for our desires, to entice and stimulate them (Jas. 1:14). If we allow him to succeed in enticing our desires, we then find ourselves dragged away by them from what we know is right. They will take us in tow, so that obeying them, we become their slaves (Titus 3:3), being led about by them. Then desire conceives and grows (Jas. 1:15); Cain, for example, was given a warning by God about the growing nature of sin (Gen. 4:7). If desire is unchecked, it gives birth to sin—David, sadly and tragically, found that to be the case when he did not check his desire when he was tempted by the sight of an attractive woman whom he discovered to be another man's wife (2 Sam. 11:2-5). As Thomas à Kempis put it, "First there cometh to mind a bare thought of evil, then a strong imagination thereof, afterward a delight and evil motive, and then consent." When sin is full-grown, it "gives birth to death" (Jas. 1:15). It separates us from God, and it brings its own dreadful penalties at the final judgment.

The time to deal with temptations, therefore, is in their beginnings. Desires and passions grow as rivers do, greater and greater the further they are carried from their spring and source. They are like rust which, left to itself, eats away unceasingly. The time to deal with rust is in its beginnings; and the same is true with temptations. They must be nipped in the bud if we are to overcome them. There is an ancient Chinese proverb which says, "We cannot prevent the black birds of evil flying over our heads, but we can prevent them from building their nests in our hair." We need to control carefully our desires, and that means being honest enough to begin with the discipline of our mind, upon what we allow our minds to dwell (1 Pet. 1:13; see also Phil. 4:8).

We need to be watchful too concerning Satan's bait, especially what he sets before our eyes. Henry Martyn, one of the early missionaries to India, visiting London as a young man found it a great contrast from Cambridge where he had studied as a student. He wrote, "How many temptations there are in the streets of London. I made a covenant with my eyes, which I kept strictly, though I was astonished to find the difficulty I had in doing this." We must be honest with ourselves about our inner desires. The responsibility rests fairly and squarely upon us.

We are not to put the blame for our temptations on God but rather on our own evil desires which we all too easily pamper. Bishop Taylor Smith, who was chaplain-general to the British army, was very blunt with men who gave the impression that when it came to temptation and their response to it they could not help being like the flotsam and jetsam carried hither and thither by the tide. "If you go to Portsmouth," he said, "you will see ships going East and ships going West, and only one wind driving both. When men say to me, they cannot help themselves falling, I reply:

'One ship drives East, one ship drives West
By the self-same wind that blows;
It's the set of the sails, and not the gales,
Which determines the way it goes.' "

We nip our temptations in the bud if we immediately call upon God for help as we see the temptation coming. Think of a spider in the middle of his web. He sits and feels the smallest fly and kills it. Prayer keeps watch at the center of our hearts in a similar fashion and is able to kill the first approach of temptation. Prayer is our best protection against temptation (Mark 14:38).

Something of Which to Be Sure

Satan tries to tell us untruths about God and to insinuate lies about Him. He would love us to think that our temptations come from God and not from our own desires enticed by Satan. But we must not be deceived either by our deceitful fallen nature or by Satan's insinuations (Jas. 1:16). In times of temptation our task is to believe God's sure Word rather than the devil.

All that we know of God emphasizes that *He is never the source of anything evil but always of everything good* (1:17). It is all too easy to try to transfer the responsibility for our sins to others. Some may even attempt to cast a slur upon God by saying, "God is tempting me," or "God deliberately put me in this position." Or we may put the blame onto Satan, neglecting to reproach ourselves for our sad lack of control over our desires.

However evil comes at us, it never comes from God. Instead, all good comes from Him, for He is the ultimate source of every good and perfect gift, without exception. God's gifts are a lovely reflection of His character: He is both good and perfect, and so, therefore, are His gifts.

Furthermore, *God Himself is unchanging.* James enjoys using vivid illustrations from nature. He has already used the sea and the wind as pictures of change, movement and instability (1:6). He has employed the sun and the wild flower and its blossom to illustrate the fleeting nature of man's material wealth. He now uses the picture of the constellations. God is "the Father of the heavenly lights, who does not change like shifting shadows" (1:17). God is the Creator of the heavenly bodies which give light to the universe and are vital to the maintenance of physical light. They seem to be among the most constant things. Yet, in fact, they have their own changes, variations and shadows. God, who made them, however, is entirely different from them—He does not change. There is no inconsistency with Him. All earthly things and, in fact, all created things are marked by change. But with God Himself, the Almighty Creator, there is no change. He is unchanging in both His character and His gifts.

New Birth

One of God's most wonderful gifts is new birth through our Lord Jesus Christ. That new birth comes about "through the word of truth" (Jas. 1:18)—a word that is as unchanging as God Himself. When we first obeyed the word of truth as it proclaimed the good news of the Lord Jesus to us, we were "born again, not of perishable seed, but of imperishable, through the living and enduring word of God" (1 Pet. 1:23).

Our spiritual new birth is a good and perfect gift from above. It has as one of its principal objects that we should be pleasing to God, and that must mean holiness of life, which in turn includes active resistance on our part to temptation and victory over it. From the sowing of God's Word in our lives, both at the beginning of our Christian life and then regularly as we receive God's instruction through the Scriptures, there grows the harvest of God's choice. We may be specific about this harvest for it is the fruit of the Spirit, the character of Jesus Christ reproduced in us (Gal. 5:22,23).

James knew that the early Christians to whom he wrote were already demonstrating in their lives the reality of the spiritual harvest—a harvest of holiness. They were the delightful first specimens of God's new creation (Jas. 1:18). As we read, for example, of the early Christians in the Acts of the Apostles and the lives of holiness and love that they lived, they are helpful models and examples for us to emulate.

We catch a small glimpse here of what God is doing in the world at this present time: He is bringing into being His new creation in Jesus Christ. He is calling out men and women of all nations and peoples to be His very own people as they believe and obey the gospel of His Son. They give proof of their being part of this new creation by the kind of life they live, and not least by their *perseverance* in the face of trials and temptations. The day is coming when God will wrap up this present creation (Heb. 1:10-12) and reveal the new. As Paul affirms, "The creation waits in eager expectation for the sons of God to be revealed" (Rom. 8:19). And so do we!

If we agree there is no sin in being wealthy, but that the key issue is our employment of our wealth, what are the everyday priorities to be followed in the use of our money and material possessions?

Our spiritual enemy, the devil, knows only too well how to entice us by our desires. What practical steps can we take to safeguard ourselves from unnecessary temptation?

If in the Acts of the Apostles we have "the first specimens of God's new creation," in what ways are the early Christians examples to us, especially when faced with trials? (See, for example, Acts 5:41,42; 7:54-60; 16:22-25.)

Four

RECEIVING THE WORD
James 1:19-27

God's Word must be taught and preached. That's a matter of urgent necessity. But if the process stops there little has been accomplished. God's Word must be received and then *acted upon* if it is to be effective in our lives. The Sermon on the Mount ends with the telling story of the two builders, one wise and the other foolish (Matt. 7:24-27). The fundamental lesson of that story is that it is not enough to hear God's Word; it must be properly received—and received with *obedience*. James's letter echoes much of the Sermon on the Mount.

The Word by which God has brought about our new birth (Jas. 1:18; see also 1 Pet. 1:23) is the identical Word by which He chooses to accomplish our spiritual growth. Healthy examples of God's new creation (Jas 1:18) are always the fruit of God's Word being effectively sown in human lives. This principle has been the consistent secret of spiritual prosperity. "Be careful to obey all the law my servant Moses gave you," God instructed Joshua; "do not turn from it to the right or to the left, that you may be successful wherever you go. Do not let this Book of the Law depart from your mouth; meditate on it day and night, so that you may be careful to do everything written in it. Then you will be prosperous and successful" (Josh. 1:7,8). David asked, "How can a young man keep his way pure?" and he then answered his own question, "By living according to your word" (Ps. 119:9).

The Right Soil

God wants our lives to produce practical righteousness (Jas. 1:19-21), and this intention is the key to understanding this passage. Our new birth is a new birth to righteousness (1 John 2:29). Our Saviour died for us "so that we might die to sins and live for righteousness" (1 Pet. 2:24). God's purpose is that we might be "filled with the fruit of righteousness" (Phil. 1:11). In the well-known parable of the sower, our Lord Jesus identified God's Word as the seed; and the crop that He wants to bring forth from the seed sown in good soil is the crop of righteousness.

It is an observable fact that the sowing of the same seed does not produce an identically fruitful crop from all soils—the fault plainly being with the soil rather than with the seed, and our Lord's explanation of the parable confirmed this (Mark 4:13-20). A group of Christians in a church fellowship may sit under the same spiritual teaching ministry week by week, and whereas some will grow spiritually, others will make little or no progress. The fault hinges upon the varying conditions of soil found in believers' souls.

Soil can be fouled or infected so that produce will not mature in it as it ought. A soil can be acidic or alkaline so that certain things will not grow in it until the acidity or alkalinity is corrected. There are spiri-

tual parallels when we come to consider the right
state of the soil of our souls for the reception of God's
Word.

There are attitudes and forms of behavior which
make it difficult—and sometimes impossible—for us
to receive God's Word as we ought. *The first harmful
attitude is anger* (Jas. 1:19,20). Anger completely
ruins the soul's soil for the Word. Anger belongs to
our old life rather than to our new (Col 3:8). It is in
opposition to the self-control which the Spirit would
encourage in us (Gal. 5:23). If ever we have gone to
church angry or having just lost our temper, we shall
know how little we have been able to concentrate on
God's Word and how little, if anything, we have
received from what has been taught and preached.

The second fouling factor is moral filth (Jas.
1:21). There is moral filth just as there is physical
filth. If I work in my attic or garden I may soon
become *physically* dirty. If I engage in silly conversation with those of the opposite sex, or watch sugges-
tive films, or read books which sell well because they
make much of sex, I'll soon find myself *morally* filthy.
By fouling the soil of my soul in this way, I'll make a
proper response to God's Word impossible. There's
many a Christian who gets little from God's Word on
a Sunday because he has fouled his soul by staying
up late on a Saturday night to watch an unhelpful
late-night movie.

*The third fouling factor is what we may describe
as prevalent evil*—"the evil that is so prevalent" (Jas.
1:21). We are not being hard or condemnatory when
we declare this age in which we live to be evil—that is
the Bible's assessment (Gal. 1:4; Eph. 5:16). The
world pressurizes us all the time to accept its standards, and to agree that if an attitude or form of
behavior is normal or usual then it must be acceptable. But our duty is to test every attitude and action
by the standards of God's Word. For example, con-

temporary standards of marital faithfulness may be far lower than those God demands. In our place of employment, we may find that it is not the norm to be scrupulously honest in the use of our employer's time and possessions. If the Christian fails to resist these pressures and simply does what everyone else does, rather than standing out for what is right, he fouls the soil of his heart by "the evil that is so prevalent."

We make no progress in spiritual growth until we learn to recognize sin honestly for what it is: moral filth and evil. It is only when we see sin in its true colors that we see the necessity of ridding ourselves of it—and it is for this that James argues when he writes, "Get rid of all moral filth and the evil that is so prevalent" (Jas. 1:21).

There are obvious reasons why anger, moral filth and prevalent evil foul the heart's soil. James spells out one for us: "man's anger does not bring about the righteous life that God desires" (1:20). If we compare the acts of the sinful nature (Gal. 5:19-21) with the fruit of the Spirit (Gal. 5:22,23), anger can fit only into the acts of the sinful nature, precisely the things on account of which our Lord Jesus Christ died for us and from which He died to deliver us. Anger so easily runs away with us and leads to other sins. A woman once told Billy Sunday, the American evangelist, that she had a bad temper, but at least it was over in a minute. His apt reply was, "So is a shotgun blast! It is over in a second, but look at the damage it can do."

God's holy character must inevitably be in opposition to anger, moral filth and prevalent evil. Born into God's spiritual family (Jas. 1:18), we must bear the family likeness. Saved by the grace of the righteous God, who through faith imputes to us the righteousness of His Son Jesus Christ (Rom. 1:17), we are committed to righteousness. A necessary consequence of our redemption is the desire to "offer the parts of our body to [God] as instruments of righteousness" (Rom. 6:13); we "have been set free from sin" so as to become the willing and happy "slaves to righteousness" (Rom. 6:18). As a man may name his hobby or favorite occupation as his "pursuit," so righteousness is to be our pursuit.

Anything contrary to righteousness fouls the soil of our hearts. We must rid ourselves, therefore, of *all* such things (Jas. 1:21). The words "get rid of" could also be translated "put off" as in the putting on or taking off of clothes. Clothes are frequently a picture of Christian behavior in the idea of putting off and putting on (Rom. 13:12; Eph. 4:22-24; Col. 3:9,10; Heb. 12:1; 1 Pet. 2:1). James may be reminding his readers of their baptism, since there is evidence that in some parts of the early church the procedure was to use clothes symbolically at that important moment of Christian initiation. As a believer went into the river to be baptized, he divested himself of certain outer garments—a picture of his putting off the sinful attitudes and actions of his old life. On the other side of the river, his Christian friends stood with some new garment or garments for him to wear—a picture of the new attitudes and behavior he was to follow because of his union with the Lord Jesus. This likely practice probably explains why the words "put off" and "put on" are Christian catchwords in the New Testament.

So far we have been dealing with negative factors, with the soil-fouling diseases of the soul. But like natural soil, the soul's soil can be prepared for the seed so that it is given a good reception and obtains the proper growth of which it is capable. We must want our souls to be the right soil for righteousness. The Word of truth (Jas. 1:18) is completely contrary in its influence to moral filth and the evil with which we are surrounded—it perfectly reflects the character of its Author, the *Holy* Spirit.

Our souls become good soil for the Word as we strive after *good relationships*. This important principle is behind James's exhortation, "Everyone should be quick to listen, slow to speak and slow to become angry" (1:19). If we ponder for a moment the kinds of things that spoil our human relationships, we shall probably agree that faults such as our indifference to others and their opinions, our slowness to listen, and our over-eagerness to put across our own point of view have something to do with it. Relationships can be ruined in a second by an outburst of anger, so that a friendship established over many years is destroyed in a moment.

We are to cultivate, therefore, those attitudes which build up good relationships. We may wonder at first why James begins like this in dealing with his subject of how to receive the Word of God properly. But the clue is this: there is a relationship between our readiness to receive advice and counsel from others, and our readiness to receive God's Word and counsel. We cannot be in a right relationship with God—so as to receive the benefits of His Word—if we are in a wrong relationship with others (1 Pet. 2:1-3). The Christian who is genuinely willing to listen to others and to receive advice as much as to give it, is likely to adopt the same attitude before God; and vice versa.

Our souls become good soil for the Word as we *accept it with humility* (Jas. 1:21). It does not matter who the teacher or preacher is, providing he faithfully declares the Word of God; we are to accept its authority, and receive it gladly, approving its goodness. We are not to sit in judgment over the Word of God; rather we are to let it sit in judgment over us. We are not to pick and choose proudly what we think we want from the Word of God; rather we are to acknowledge humbly that we need all of its instruction.

Our souls become good soil for the Word as we *rec-*

ognize its power to save (1:21). We may be puzzled at
first by the way James expresses himself here,
because we know that it is God alone who can save
us. But it is the Word *of God* of which James speaks.
To our Western way of thinking, words can be in
opposition to action. We may sometimes declare of
what a person says, "Well, it's *only* words!" But such
is not true when we speak of God's Word. What God
says, He does! Paul instructs us too that the Holy
Scriptures are able to make us "wise for salvation
through faith in Christ Jesus" (2 Tim. 3:15), because
they are "God-breathed" (2 Tim. 3:16).

We must not overlook the importance of testing
the soil which our souls present to God's Word: "My
dear brothers," James writes, "take note of this . . ."
(1:19). We all need to heed this counsel—there are no
exceptions. It is necessary at times to take a soil-test.
Is my soul's soil fouled or diseased? Perhaps by
anger, moral filth or other prevalent evils? Or is my
soul's soil ready for God's Word because I am striving
after good relationships, humility and honest submission to the authority of God's Word?

The Right Response

It is not enough to receive the Word well; it must
then be *obeyed* (Jas. 1:22-25). God's Word demands
a response; it is God's voice speaking to us. Whenever
God's Word comes to us, there is a sense in which we
can never be exactly the same again. We always make
some kind of response; insofar that even an apparent
"no response" is really a negative response—a repuls-
ing of the Word so that we inevitably move backwards
rather than forwards.

The way we listen is vitally important. To echo the
Old Testament, we need to turn our ear to wisdom, to
apply our heart to understanding, to call out for
insight, to cry aloud to God for understanding, and
to look for it as a man searches for hidden treasure

that he knows is there to be found (Prov. 2:1-5).

But listening on its own is not enough (Jas. 1:22). To listen and then to do nothing to implement what we hear is to deceive ourselves as to any profit we may think that we are receiving from the preaching of God's Word. We may make ourselves "Word-hardened." It is possible to become "sermon-proof" so that the truths which once struck home no longer register because we have not accompanied our understanding of them with obedience. The right response to God's Word, whenever we hear it, is *obedience*— doing what it says (1:22).

James uses the picture of God's Word as a mirror (1:23; see also 2 Cor. 3:18). A mirror brings both people and things before our physical eyes, and the Bible likewise brings both God Himself in Christ and spiritual realities, before the eyes of our understanding. A mirror shows us what we really look like, and the Bible shows us the truth about ourselves—every spot and blemish—as no other mirror. Sometimes, sadly, it has to show us to ourselves as "wretched, pitiful, poor, blind and naked" (Rev. 3:17). We use a mirror to dress ourselves, as we check that everything is in place, and the Bible, like a mirror, helps us to ensure that we have "put off" the clothes of our old life and have "put on" the clothes of our new life in Christ.

But a mirror is no use unless we take notice of what it reveals! To only listen—that is to say, to stop at just hearing the Word—is "like a man who looks at his face in a mirror and, after looking at himself, goes away and immediately forgets what he looks like" (Jas. 1:23,24).

To give the right response to God's Word as a mirror, there are three things we must do. *First, we must look intently into it* (1:25). The verb James employs implies looking carefully into something. In other words, we are not to come to the Word of God casually. As we are brought face to face with its truths, we are to look into them, investigate them, and ensure that we understand their relevance and practical application to life. Some of us may be used to studying and to applying a whole range of principles to everyday situations in our work. The standard of application and seriousness we give to study in other spheres must be the minimum standard we are prepared to give to God's Word.

Second, we are to look into God's Word continually. It is something we are to *continue* to do (1:25). There is no place in the Christian life for occasional reading and study of the Bible—it is to be a daily *practice.* It is to be meditated upon day and night (Josh. 1:8). Like David, if we are spiritually healthy, we shall be saying, "Oh, how I love your law! I meditate on it all day long" (Ps. 119:97). We need to cultivate a sustained looking at God's Word.

Third, we are to cultivate an unforgettable looking at God's Word (Jas. 1:25). If as Christians we lived in the good of all that we have heard from God's Word, what a revolution would take place in our lives, and what a difference it would make to our testimonies! We are to make looking and doing synonymous. We are to aim at matching every look at the Bible with obedience. *Looking and obeying*—that's what God wants from us as we look into the mirror of His Word. Once again James is reflecting our Lord's concluding story in the Sermon on the Mount of the two builders (Matt. 7:24-27).

A right response to God's Word brings God's blessing, "he will be blessed in what he does" (Jas. 1:25). Obedience draws to itself God's blessing. Hearing *plus* obedience *equals* blessing—and that spiritual arithmetic really is the secret of successful Christian living. Part of the blessing is the freedom that God's perfect law provides as it is obeyed. God's children are intended to know the most glorious freedom (Rom. 8:21), since it is for freedom that our Lord

Jesus has set us free (Gal. 5:1). But, significantly, our freedom—whether from guilt, lust, fear, loneliness, and aimlessness—is dependent upon our obedience, our holding on to what we are taught. "To the Jews who had believed him, Jesus said, 'If you hold to my teaching, you are really my disciples. Then you will know the truth, and the truth will set you free' " (John 8:31,32). It is only by obeying the truth of God's Word that we really know its power in experience, and that experience itself then leads on to further knowledge of the truth.

The Right Proof

Truth is often made clearer by appropriate illustration, and so James provides an illustration of the difference between mere listening and listening *and* doing (Jas. 1:26,27). There is, on the one hand, a religion which allows a man to be so self-satisfied that he is content with holding views and convictions without any feeling of responsibility to exercise self-control or to become involved in the urgent needs of others. On the other hand, there is the religious profession that an obedient Christian makes which deflates his feelings of self-importance and makes him concerned to be in control of himself and to be involved in meeting the needs of those around him.

James does not avoid using the word "religion" as we might perhaps be inclined to do. Religion is basically the manner in which men think they may honor God and worship Him. James is not trying to provide a complete definition of religion here. While he tells us what true religion is, he is not trying to tell us *all* that it is but he is explaining what it is in relation to what he has just been emphasizing about obedience to God's Word.

The man who "considers himself religious" and who stops at listening without going on to obedience "does not keep a tight rein on his tongue" (1:26).

Obedience to God is the rein which controls the tongue. (James is going to have much more to say about the tongue in chapter 3.) Religious profession that does not control a man's use of his tongue is self-deceiving and worthless (1:26). A religion of words—of words without practice—has no value to God or to our fellowman.

But true religion—that which "God our Father accepts as pure and faultless" (1:27)—is quite different. It is a consequence of new birth (1:18), and, as we have said earlier, it is a new birth to righteousness because of our adoption into God's family and our union with the Lord Jesus Christ. Our Lord Jesus "went around doing good" (Acts 10:38), and our union with Him, made real by God's indwelling Spirit, means that we want His mind to be in us (Phil. 2:5) so that we begin to do the same. As we both receive and obey the Word of God, this determination to be like our Lord Jesus becomes a reality in practice.

James pinpoints three examples of obedience which are the right kind of proof to expect if we are giving God's Word its right reception. *First, there will be an increase in self-control.* Some, temperamentally, are able to exercise self-control more readily than others. But as Christians, this is to be a growing virtue in us all. Part of self-control—and of true religion—is keeping a tight rein on our tongue.

Second, there will be a genuine social concern—a looking after of "orphans and widows in their distress" (1:27), and they serve to symbolize all human need. Orphans are a particular object of God's concern. Believers, significantly, call God "Father" (1:27), and it is because we know God to be the Father "from whom the whole family of believers in heaven and on earth derives its name" (Eph. 3:15), that we know that He cares for orphans. The Lord Jesus promised that He would not leave His disciples as orphans (John 14:18). Reflecting God's image and our Saviour's compassion, we shall be concerned for them and others in similar conditions. Widowhood is also a time of distress and those who are in a right relationship with God, through their obedience to His Word and gospel, actively sympathize with them and go to their rescue.

Third, there will be spiritual watchfulness so that we keep ourselves "from being polluted by the world" (1:27). The word *world* is used here in the sense of the world lost in sin, wholly at odds in its spirit and attitudes to the things of God. We are in the world but we are no longer part of the world because of our heavenly citizenship and commitment to the Lord Jesus. The standards of our new life are those of heaven, not those of the society around us. The world, dominated by Satan, constantly strives to capture our hearts by playing upon our natural physical cravings, by capturing our eyes to encourage lust, and by making us want to boast about our possessions (1 John 2:16). But the one unfailing corrective to worldliness and pollution by the spirit and attitudes of the world is regular exposure to God's Word, coupled with obedience to it. Our right response to the Word of God, and the proof of it, is righteousness—and that righteousness is one of the chief evidences that we are part of God's new creation (Jas. 18,20; see also Rom. 14:17).

We ought to notice, in passing, that James does not limit religion to genuine social concern, but links it with self-control and spiritual watchfulness. Hannah More, the English writer and philanthropist, emphasized that some, sadly, made "benevolence a substitute for Christianity." "It seems to be one of the reigning errors among some to reduce all religion into almsgiving."

"The proof of the pudding is in the eating" is what we sometimes say about cooking. *The proof of the hearing is in the obeying*—that's what we must say about our hearing and receiving of God's Word. As someone has said, "If you want the world to heed, put your creed into your deed."

If we are to rid ourselves of moral filth and prevalent evils, we must be honest enough to identify them. In what ways do we find ourselves coming into contact with moral filth and being influenced by prevalent evils? And what can we do to avoid them, where such avoidance is possible?

How can we avoid the snare of simply listening to the Word out of habit without the habit of obedience?

"Orphans and widows" summed up some of the principal social needs of the first century when James wrote. What are the main social needs in which Christians must be involved now?

Five

FAVORITISM
James 2:1-13

When you and I write letters, we don't write them in chapters! It's important to remember that James didn't do so either, and the chapter divisions are provided for our convenience, for our ease of reference. James's present subject, although different in its application, is the same as at the end of chapter 1—obedience to God's Word. *Listen and do*—that has been James's plea (1:22). Listening without obedience is unprofitable listening. It may even become a dangerous listening because we may become hardened in our indifference and disobedience. James's great desire for God's people is that they should be always looking intently into God's Word—"the perfect law that gives freedom" (1:25)—whether by reading it for themselves or by hearing it taught and preached, and *at the same time* putting it into practice.

Having applied this principle to caring for orphans and widows and the duty of the Christian to keep himself "from being polluted by the world" (1:27), James takes up a subject of particular relevance to his first-century readers in order to ram home again the importance of practical obedience to God's Word—and the subject is favoritism. Favoritism is the inclination to show undue preference to respect to someone. It is essentially something that we "show" to people by giving them "special attention" (2:3).

Favoritism may not seem to be a particularly relevant subject to our contemporary situation, but we may be in for a surprise! First, we must appreciate the background of James's readers. They tended to be either wealthy or poor—there were few in-between stages. In Western society, the majority of people tend to be in-between—we may not be rich but we are certainly not poor. That was not the case in the first century. The church from the beginning was made up, for the most part, of poorer people. Such a state of affairs is implied in this passage since James writes to his readers assuming that the majority of them might be categorized as "the poor" (1:9; 2:5,6). Paul urged the Corinthian Christians: "Brothers, think of what you were when you were called. Not many of you were wise by human standards; not many were influential; not many were of noble birth" (1 Cor. 1:26). Speaking generally, there were far more poor people in the church than rich. There was nothing surprising in this: there were far more poor people in society than rich, and so there were more poor people than wealthy in need of salvation. Furthermore, poverty may cause a man to face up to his need of God's gracious help, whereas a rich man may be lulled into a false sense of security, saying to himself, "I am rich; I have acquired wealth and do not need a thing" (Rev. 3:17). The fact that the majority of early believers were poor must not obscure the fact that there were also believers from wealthy backgrounds. Furthermore, rich individuals came into Christian assemblies from time to time because they were seeking after the truth.

The rich were identifiable, even as they are in our own society. In the first century, they could be recognized by the gold rings on their fingers and the superior quality clothes they wore (Jas. 2:2). The mistake of some Christians was to make a fuss of the wealthy when they identified themselves in any way with the church. They treated them as "important." Carnal, earthly reasoning came into operation—it might pay off to be considerate to them. Not all could be comfortably seated in the church's meeting place, and so the rich were offered the good seats (2:3). Now it is never wrong to be considerate of people and to want to provide them with the best, but these commendable things become wrong when we deliberately give them to some and deny them to others. The attention the Christians gave at the door to the rich was not given to the poor. The poor man was noticeable by the absence of jewelry and smart clothes. In fact, he might have been shabby and even smelly! Rather than ensuring that he too was comfortably seated, the attitude was, "Well, you can either stand or sit on the floor" (2:3).

James points out how that on the merely human level such preferential treatment does not make sense. If people deserve to be honored on account of merit or commendable actions, that is appropriate. But wealth does not in and of itself deserve honor. Wealth may not always have been obtained honorably, and it may not be used in a God-pleasing manner. Furthermore, it was the rich in first-century society who exploited the poor, and who, in the pursuit of their exploitation, took them to court to extract all they could from them financially (2:6,7). More important still, some of the rich thought nothing of blaspheming the name of the Lord Jesus (2:7), the name the believer loves above every other name.

The Christian's life is to be free from favoritism,

and it should find no place within the corporate life of God's people. The local church is to be perhaps the one place where men and women may be sure that all wrongful human barriers are broken down, and where the acceptance God Himself gives to men and women is reflected in our acceptance of one another.

Perhaps we need to be careful in case we dismiss this problem of the early church in regard to the rich as being of little relevance to us in our church or fellowship. Attention to wealth is not an unknown temptation to us. If a church member is known to be particularly wealthy, it is sadly possible for the church to give more attention to what that wealthy individual thinks about some idea or project—especially if finance is involved—than to what someone less affluent thinks. In the world at large, wealth so often equals influence; but that ought not to be the case in the local church. Church elders or deacons act foolishly if they give preference to the views of certain individuals simply because they are wealthy. Such favoritism and carnality are displeasing to God.

But there are other false grounds for favoritism than wealth, such as status or intelligence. The time arises in most local churches when officers, elders and deacons have to be appointed. Significantly, the New Testament emphasizes that the most important qualifications are qualifications of character (1 Tim. 3:1-13; Titus 1:5-9)—in fact, Christlikeness. But favoritism enters in when, instead of being guided by the standards laid down in the Bible, we vote according to a person's status, or intelligence and education, or friendship.

Perhaps the unspoken argument goes something like this: "He's a very prominent man in his profession—it would be good to have him in leadership in the church." Now it is true that it is excellent when a man's natural gifts can be put to use in the local church, but spirituality and spiritual gifts count most of all when it comes to holding office. We are all naturally pleased when people who are our friends are nominated for office within the church, but the exercise of our vote on their behalf must not be on the grounds of friendship alone, for that is simply favoritism. Sometimes true friendship may mean that we say to our friend, "I'm not convinced that now is the Lord's timing for you to hold office, and I'll be voting for someone else."

We must not allow ourselves to forget that this whole subject arises from James's concern that his readers should obey the Word—that they should not simply listen to it but they must do it. The basic question we need to ask, therefore, is, "How does looking into God's perfect law affect our attitude to things such as favoritism?"

The Mind of Christ

Obedience to God's Word is synonymous with striving to have the same attitude as that of our Saviour, the Lord Jesus Christ (see Phil. 2:5-18). James begins what he has to say on this subject of favoritism by reminding his readers that they are "believers in our glorious Lord Jesus Christ" (2:1). Literally, James describes our Saviour as *the Glory*—the implication being that our Lord Jesus is the presence of God manifested with His people, as the Shekinah was the divine presence dwelling among the Israelites in earlier times. The term *Lord* also raises Him above the human level and reminds us of His dignity as the Son of God, the second Person of the Trinity. The thrust of James's words, "My brothers, as believers in our glorious Lord Jesus Christ, don't show favoritism" is plainly a plea to behave in regard to wealth and poverty exactly as did our Lord Jesus Christ.

His wealth is unimaginable—the wealth of glory—but He laid it all aside for our sakes. As Paul wrote, "You know the grace of our Lord Jesus Christ, that though he was rich, yet for your sakes he became poor, so that you through his poverty might become rich" (2 Cor. 8:9). The Lord Jesus has revealed to us that real wealth is not money in the bank but treasure in heaven. When our Saviour was here on earth He would have been counted among the poor rather than the wealthy. As the Son of man He had "no place to lay his head" (Matt. 8:20). In His dealings with men and women, He gave Himself equally to all, and the poor were left in no doubt of His concern and identity with them. Part of the message John the Baptist's disciples took back to him in prison from the Lord Jesus was: "Go back and report to John what you hear and see: . . . the good news is preached to the poor" (Matt. 11:4,5).

Furthermore, the Lord Jesus taught that in caring for the needy—and in particular for the poor—we care for Him: "For I was hungry and you gave me something to eat, I was thirsty and you gave me something to drink, I was a stranger and you invited me in, I needed clothes and you clothed me, I was sick and you looked after me, I was in prison and you came to visit me" (Matt. 25:35,36).

James is saying, in effect, "You believe in the Lord Jesus, the Lord of glory, don't you? Well, then, follow His example, and obey the teaching He gave about wealth and concern for the poor. If you really believe in Him, then you will want to have His mind in you."

The Lord Jesus never looked at a man's outward appearance and assessed a man's worth by it. Rather He looked at all men with love and saw them as those whom He longed to serve. To show favoritism and to be snobbish are contrary attitudes because they mean that we classify people in our minds, and we make false assumptions concerning them on the ground of their appearance. In fact, we set ourselves up as judges to assess others, forgetful of the Saviour's warning: "Do not judge, or you too will be judged. For in the same way you judge others, you will be judged, and with the measure you use, it will be measured to you" (Matt. 7:1,2).

Obedience to the Word of God produces a determination to have the same attitude towards people as that of our Lord Jesus Christ, and that attitude rules out all favoritism and snobbishness.

Invisible Realities

Obedience to God's Word means that our reactions to both people and possessions are governed by invisible realities rather than by visible considerations of doubtful value. Those Christians who stood at the door of the Christian meeting place and gave a different kind of welcome to the wealthy than to the poor were governed by human considerations. Obedience to the Word would have led them to be governed by the invisible realities of the gospel of "our glorious Lord Jesus Christ."

First, there is the invisible reality of God's election: "Has not God *chosen* those who are poor in the eyes of the world to be rich in faith and to inherit the kingdom he promised those who love him?" (Jas. 2:5). Election is God's eternal, unconditional choice of guilty sinners to be redeemed and born again of His Spirit so that they may be brought finally to His everlasting glory. The Lord Jesus said to His disciples, "You did not choose me, but I chose you" (John 15:16). There is a mystery about God's choice, but one thing is absolutely plain—it has no regard at all to any works or merit on the believer's part (Rom. 11:6; 2 Tim. 1:9). What is equally certain is that God has chosen to call as many poor as rich, if not more.

Second, there is the invisible reality of faith and also of faith's wealth (Jas. 2:5). Faith itself is a precious gift of God (Eph. 2:8). Faith begins as an act by which a person abandons reliance on himself to merit salvation, has a firm conviction as to the truth of God's promises of mercy in the Lord Jesus, and depends sincerely upon them. After this, faith becomes a habit of that person's life. Now this precious gift of faith is given to rich and poor alike. The gospel was, and is, preached to the poor (Matt. 11:5) in order that they might believe and enter into the spiritual wealth God bestows on those who trust in His glorious Son.

It may be that the only thing in which a man is rich is faith, but if so he is rich in the commodity that matters most because "without faith it is impossible to please God, because anyone who comes to him must believe that he exists and that he rewards those who earnestly seek him" (Heb. 11:6). Faith makes a man rich towards God (Luke 12:21) because it brings him into living union with the risen and glorious Lord Jesus (Gal. 2:20). If, therefore, we would know who the "wealthiest" members of our church fellowship are—as God sees it—we should look at the faith of men and women, for that invisible reality is more valuable than all the world's money and possessions.

Third, there is the invisible reality of God's kingdom (Jas. 2:5). The kingdom of God, or the kingdom of heaven, is spoken of in two ways in the Bible: first, as that of which Christians are members because the Lord Jesus, through the new birth (John 3:3,5), actively rules in their hearts; and second, as that which they possess as an inheritance in the future (Matt. 25:34; Luke 22:16; 2 Tim. 4:18; Heb. 12:28). The greatest blessings conceivable are found in it—it is like a treasure (Matt. 13:44), or like a superb pearl worthy of a man surrendering all that he has in order to possess it (Matt. 13:45,46). God Himself calls men and women into His kingdom (1 Thess. 2:12), and, in common with election, human merit has no place in that call, for none deserve entry. The rich may have little prospect of entering into the kingdom because their wealth may become more important to them than a right relationship to God, which makes them, in fact, poor toward God and in peril of their souls' everlasting unhappiness. The members of God's kingdom cannot be discerned by the gold rings on their fingers and by the quality of their clothes, but they can be recognized by the quality of their lives (see Rom. 14:17; Gal. 5:22,23).

Fourth, there is the invisible reality of God's promises (Jas. 2:5). God has promised the kingdom, and much more besides, to those who trust in His Son. God "has given us his very great and precious promises, so that through them you may participate in the divine nature and escape the corruption in the world caused by evil desires" (2 Pet. 1:4). God regards those who believe in His Son as heirs—they are to *inherit* the kingdom. We are, therefore, heirs of God, and co-heirs with our glorious Lord (Rom. 8:17; Gal. 4:7), and all according to the promises of God "who does not lie" (Titus 1:2).

Fifth, there is the invisible reality of love for God (Jas. 2:5). God promises His kingdom to "those who love him." Their love is not itself the ground of their acceptance with Him but it is the consequence of their having discovered acceptance with God through His dear Son who died and rose again for them. "We love because he first loved us" (1 John 4:19). God delights in His children's love for Him and for His Son because it is a free and spontaneous love. The more we appreciate what it means to be forgiven, and to be reconciled to God, the more we love (Luke 7:47). But love for God cannot be recognized by gold rings and fine clothes, and so any classifying of people on such counts is false and wrong. Guided, as we ought to be, by the invisible realities of the gospel, we cannot countenance snobbishness or favoritism.

Love's Priority
Obedience to God's Word means following the way

of love (1 Cor. 14:1; Jas. 2:8). The word translated "right" (Jas. 2:8) is not the unusual word *dikaios* but *kalos*, which in this context means what is pleasing to God, what He likes or gives Him joy. *Dikaios* has more the sense of conforming to the laws of God and man, and living in accordance with them. But either word is appropriate here because James writes about the "royal law" (2:8)—"royal" because it is the law of the King of kings, and is the law which is obligatory for all who belong to His kingdom. It is the law which God has given us in the Scriptures.

James takes up one of the Old Testament summaries of the second table of the Ten Commandments, "Love your neighbor as yourself" (2:8; Lev. 19:18) and reminds his Christian readers of the priority and binding nature of this commandment. Righteousness and love go hand in hand in God's kingdom. To do the right thing and to love are the two sides of the same coin. As believers, we make it our goal to please the Lord (2 Cor. 5:9), and in order to please Him we must pursue love and aim always at doing the right thing in regard to others. To show favoritism is in total opposition to the summary of the second table of the law—"Love your neighbor as yourself"—because none of us enjoys being passed over simply because of someone's favoritism for another person.

The danger is that we may feel that favoritism is a small thing, and that it can surely be permitted in minor ways. But that attitude is a mistake, both with regard to favoritism and to any other sin. The law of God contains and consists of one indivisible principle—love. To break one commandment proves our willingness to break others or all of God's commandments, because the right motive behind obedience is love for God, and when we really love Him we don't pick and choose which commandments are acceptable. They are all equally right for us because our

Lord and King commands them all.

The principle enunciated in James 2:10 that "whoever keeps the whole law and yet stumbles at just one point is guilty of breaking all of it" is of fundamental importance. We are lawbreakers if we break only *one* of God's commandments or if we break *all* of them. Any voluntary breaking of God's law proves that our love for God is deficient.

Those who think favoritism a small thing, James implies, should think again. To show favoritism is a contradiction of the basic commandment behind all the commands of God relating to my treatment of my neighbor, and to be guilty of it is to become a lawbreaker, and to displease God (Jas. 2:9).

God's Judgment

Obedience to God's Word means that we never forget the truth that even though we are Christians we still have to face judgment (2:12). It is perfectly true that the first part of the judgment will be the separation of those who have accepted God's way of salvation from those who have gone about to gain salvation by dependence on their own efforts (Matt. 25:31-33), and that there will be no condemnation for those who are justified by faith in the Lord Jesus Christ (Rom. 5:1; 8:1). But the proof of justifying faith is works—and this is to be James's next theme—and if our faith is real, believing in the judgment, we shall "speak and act as those who are going to be judged by the law that gives freedom" (Jas. 5:12; 1:25). God's law has new meaning to us as Christians.

Having escaped the law's just penalty upon our sins through our Saviour's death in our place, we now gladly accept the duties to which God's law points because, by His indwelling Spirit, we have new resources to enable us to keep His law as never before. To try to keep God's law is not a matter of bondage because of our failures but it becomes a joy because it expresses our love to God. For example, the Lord Jesus said, "If you love me, you will obey what I command" (John 14:15). He also said, "This is my command: Love each other" (John 15:17). Love delights in mercy: "it keeps no record of wrongs, . . . does not delight in evil but rejoices with the truth. It always trusts, always hopes, always perseveres" (1 Cor. 13:5-7). Favoritism, flattering of the wealthy, and snobbishness are opposites of love because they involve—often without our realizing it—judging others and a sad failure to show compassion and mercy. In fact, where there is true Christian love it chooses to overlook faults when they are obviously present, and it deals graciously with people—"Mercy triumphs over judgment!" (Jas. 2:13).

The manner in which we deal with others—including our displays of favoritism, partiality and snobbishness (whether secret or displayed) will all influence the judgment we shall receive as the servants of our Lord Jesus when we stand before Him.

When we live in obedience to God's Word we strive to deal with others as God deals with us. That way of life not only puts to death hurtful sins like favoritism but it makes us easy to live with and glorifying to our Lord Jesus as we reflect His grace in our lives.

How real a problem is favoritism in daily life and in church life? What are the different forms it can take? In what ways is it a reflection of selfishness?

Imagine a non-Christian resists the truth that he is a sinner, saying, "There are only little things wrong in my life." How would you use verse 10 to help him understand the truth about himself and about God?

We are to "speak and act as those who are going to be judged by the law that gives freedom" (2:12). Words and actions: to which do we give the greater attention or care? In which do we sin more easily? In what ways can our words and actions be influenced by favoritism?

Six

FAITH AND WORKS
James 2:14-26

The title for this section is almost inevitable. It is the key passage in the whole of the Bible concerning the relationship of works to faith. Once more James gives us insight into the concern which prompted him to write his letter. He wrestles with a problem which always faces the church—the existence of people who profess to be believers without their really being so.

A Problem

The problem is that some people claim to have faith but they don't demonstrate the truth of that claim by the kind of lives they live. "What good is it, my brothers," James asks, "if a man claims to have faith but has no deeds? Can such faith save him?" (2:14)

The key word here is *claims*. James is not conceding that the people concerned really possess faith. What is plain is that they claim that they do. So far as James is concerned a profession of faith without accompanying deeds is a cause for alarm—it sounds warning bells in his ears. And James was right. Throughout his letter we find distinct echoes of our Lord Jesus' teaching in what we usually call the Sermon on the Mount. In that teaching our Lord likened men's lives to trees, and He made the point that a good tree bears good fruit—the fruit is the test of the tree. Applying this test to men's lives, He concluded, "Thus, by their fruit you will recognize them" (Matt. 7:20). Good works are the fruit of the tree of faith. Any profession of faith without faith's fruit must cast doubt, therefore, upon the reality of the faith that is professed.

Faith, in common with many other important words, may be used in a variety of ways. One man may say, "I have faith" and simply mean that he believes in the general possibility of God's existence. Another may declare, "I have faith" and mean that he believes that God exists and that Jesus Christ is the Son of God. But neither of these affirmations of faith is what we may describe as "saving faith"—the faith that brings a man into a saving relationship with Jesus Christ. They are not "justifying faith"—the faith that brings a man into an experience of God reckoning to him the righteousness of His Son, Jesus Christ. It is sadly possible for a person to imagine mistakenly that he has faith. Our Lord followed up His statement about a tree and its fruit by giving a warning to those who make a false profession of faith (Matt. 7:21-23).

James cannot accept faith without good works because he knew how our Lord Jesus put the two together. It is important to remember that James still has his theme of listening and doing in mind and that *faith and works* are almost synonymous with listening and obeying. The right kind of listening—the listening of faith—results in obedience—the works of faith. Caring for orphans and widows

(1:27), the avoidance of worldliness of spirit (1:27), and freedom from favoritism and snobbishness (2:1-13) are all works of genuine faith "in our glorious Lord Jesus Christ" (2:1).

James cannot accept that faith without works can save a man. He asks, "Can such faith save him?" (2:14). The introduction of the thought of faith saving a man needs a little explanation in order to avoid misunderstanding. Faith itself does not save—that is the consistent teaching of the Bible. It is the Lord Jesus Christ alone who can save—and His name declares that fact. Joseph was told by the angel, "You are to give him the name Jesus, because he will save his people from their sins" (Matt. 1:21). But faith—and only faith—brings a man or woman into a saving union with the Lord Jesus Christ. Faith—which is itself a gift of God (Eph. 2:8)—is the one thing necessary if a man or woman is to enter into the experience of salvation.

There were occasions in the gospels when the Lord Jesus said to individuals who came to Him, "Your faith has saved you." The significant feature, however, is that it seems that in each case the faith He approved was faith seen in action. He saw the faith of the four men who lowered their paralyzed friend through the roof on a mat in order to get him to Jesus—faith in action (Mark 2:1-12; see especially v. 5)! He also discerned the sincere faith of the woman who had once lived a sinful life and who came to Simon's house in order to anoint Jesus' feet (Luke 7:36-50). Her act of anointing was an activity of her grateful faith.

The Proper Conclusion

James's resolution to the problem posed by professions of faith that stand on their own without supporting works and deeds is crystal clear: "faith by itself, if it is not accompanied by action, is dead"

(2:17). True faith is lively. Where it is present, therefore, it is active in deeds. It's rather like a young
child; it cannot keep still and do nothing! On the
other hand, faith that stops at profession—mere
words—is dead, and dead faith is devoid of deeds and
is empty of action. Dead faith has no value and it
does no good. In fact, the challenging thing is that
dead faith can do harm because undiscerning people
may regard a profession of faith as identical with the
real thing, and be put off and disillusioned about
Christianity by the bad example of those who profess
to believe but whose lives do not correspond with that
profession.

James gives a practical illustration from another
sphere, that of sympathy, to show the complete use-
lessness of dead faith, of faith that stops at words.
"Suppose a brother or sister is without clothes and
daily food. If one of you says to him, 'Go, I wish you
well; keep warm and well fed,' but does nothing about
his physical needs, what good is it?" (2:15,16). If a
man is both cold and hungry, sympathy which stops
at words is dead sympathy—and so too is faith which
stops at words. James's conclusion is blunt and to
the point. It is intended to shock and to make us sit
up and check that our faith is alive and not of the
dead variety: "In the same way, faith by itself, if it is
not accompanied by action, is dead" (2:17).

An Objection

James anticipates an objection to his conclusion.
"But someone will say, 'You have faith; I have deeds' "
(2:18). The argument of this imaginary objector goes
something like this: "We are all different—and you
surely appreciate that fact. Some people happen to be
more demonstrative than others. Others of us are
more reserved. You may happen to show your faith
more in action because you are an extrovert. On the
other hand, others of us keep our faith to ourselves

more, but it's a faith for all that!"

But the argument of this imaginary objector is based upon a misconception. Faith and works *cannot* be separated when it comes to salvation. God has joined them together. It is not, therefore, a matter of some people being better at faith and others being better at works: they must go hand in hand. James challenges the approach of his imaginary objector: "Show me your faith without deeds, and I will show you my faith by what I do" (2:18). In effect, James says, "Let's get down to brass tacks. Really evaluate faith—bare faith—on its own, and then look at faith in action and see what conclusions you come to concerning the reality of them both!"

An obvious evidence that faith on its own—faith without works—is not enough is in the profession even the demons, who are under Satan's control, are able to make (2:19). They believe in God's existence and shudder with fear at the thought of His reality, but that belief does not equal saving faith—the faith that saves a man and brings him into the right relationship with God through Jesus Christ.

Two Proofs

The point James makes is so fundamental that it is important that we should be in no doubt about it. James provides, therefore, two proofs from Bible history of the vital relationship between faith and works. Perhaps he bears in mind the fact that his readership is made up of both Jewish and Gentile believers, because he uses an example of God's dealing with the most well-known figure of Jewish history and then with a non-Jewish woman.

The first proof is the experience of Abraham. He was an excellent example for James to use. Abraham was, and is, the most respected Jewish ancestor of the Hebrew people. He is regarded as the father of the Jewish people. Every true Jew regards himself as a son of Abraham. The New Testament teaches that Abraham is also the spiritual father of all who believe. In fact, spiritual birth (Jas. 1:18) is the true qualification for being a son or daughter of Abraham (Luke 19:9; Rom. 2:28,29; Gal. 3:7).

Abraham is an outstanding example of how God chooses to deal with men. Abraham found God's way of putting men right with Himself—he was considered righteous by God (Jas. 2:21). To be considered righteous is the New Testament way of expressing justification. To be saved (2:14) is to be justified (2:24), and to be justified is to be saved. We may define justification as the free and undeserved act of God by which He reckons to a sinner, through faith, the righteousness of our Lord Jesus Christ. He is then able to declare the sinner just and right before Him.

We know that Abraham, in spite of all his importance and prominence, was a sinner like ourselves. The book of Genesis, for example, honestly records his sad and repeated deception over the identity of Sarah as his wife (Gen. 12:10-20; 20:1-18). Abraham knew, and we all need to know, that no living person is righteous before the Lord (Ps. 143:2): "all have sinned and fall short of the glory of God" (Rom. 3:23).

Nevertheless the Bible declares that Abraham was reckoned or *considered* righteous by God (Jas. 2:21,23). Now he was reckoned as righteous because of his obedience to God's Law. At that stage in human history, the Law of God in the Ten Commandments had not yet been given. When Abraham deceived others about the identity of Sarah as his wife, he knowingly went against the law of God written on his heart, and his conscience bore witness (Rom. 2:15). It is perfectly true, of course, that theoretically the Law of God is a means of justification. By perfect obedience to the Law of God an individual could be justified before God (Rom. 2:13; 10:5; Lev.

18:5). But in fact all men everywhere have broken God's Law (Rom. 3:9,19; see also 9:31)—and that Law itself serves to bring home to us an awareness of sin (Rom. 3:20). Abraham was as guilty of disobedience as we are.

But Abraham was justified! He was reckoned righteous by God on account of *faith*. James quotes Genesis 15:6: "Abraham believed God, and it was credited to him as righteousness," and he goes on to add, "and he was called God's friend" (Jas. 2:23).

If we pause to ponder what James says we can see the relevance of what he endeavors to teach. How do we know that Abraham's faith was not merely profession, and no more—the very things about which James has been concerned (2:14)? The answer is straightforward: Abraham's faith was proved to be genuine faith—justifying faith—by his works. One work of faith in particular is quoted: "he offered his son Isaac on the altar" (2:21).

The writer to the Hebrews uses this same incident as an illustration of Abraham's faith: "By faith Abraham, when God tested him, offered Isaac as a sacrifice. He who had received the promises was about to sacrifice his one and only son, even though God had said to him, 'It is through Isaac that your offspring will be reckoned.' Abraham reasoned that God could raise the dead, and figuratively speaking, he did receive Isaac back from death" (Heb. 11:17-19). Abraham's faith and action worked hand in hand together (Jas. 2:22). His faith, for example, reasoned that God could raise the dead. It did not then stop there. It resulted in his action in actually binding Isaac to the altar, and preparing to kill him, in keeping with his confidence that God had the power to give him Isaac back again. Abraham's faith was made complete—it was demonstrated to be the real thing—"by what he did" (2:22). As William Tyndale, the great translator of the English Bible put it, "Faith justified Abraham, and was the mother of all his good works which he afterwards did."

It is interesting that James takes up the Old Testament description of Abraham as God's friend (2:23; see also Isa. 41:8) because he was proved God's friend by our Lord's own criterion: "You are my friends if you do what I command" (John 15:14). Abraham's obedience—which was the activity of his faith—pleased God (Heb. 11:8,9,17), and it is this kind of obedience, the obedience of faith, which concerns James (as in 1:22). James sees the conclusion to be drawn from Abraham's example as indisputable: "You see that a person is justified by what he does and not by faith alone" (2:24).

Verse 24 must be read in the light of the fact that James has quoted and accepted completely the statement of Genesis 15:6 that "Abraham believed God, and it was credited to him as righteousness" (2:23). He is not disputing for a moment the fundamental doctrine of justification by faith.

But some have thought that he is at variance with the apostle Paul on this subject of faith and works. Luther, for example, whose whole life had been transformed by the truth of justification by faith as he had studied and expounded Paul's New Testament letters, regarded James as an "epistle of straw" because it seemed to him that James's emphasis is opposed to Paul's. But such a view is a result of misunderstanding.

In dealing with the subject of faith and works, Paul and James are saying the same thing, only they come to the subject from different angles because of the particular pastoral situations with which they are dealing.

When Paul handles the subject of justification he is concerned to point out that justification—which equals salvation—cannot be achieved by works. It can come to a man solely through the finished work of our Lord Jesus Christ on the cross, and it must be entered into by faith.

When James deals with the subject of justification, however, he is concerned to point out that justification by faith is so radical in its consequences in a person's experience that it results in works that prove its existence and vitality. When we believe and trust in our Lord Jesus Christ and His finished atoning work, our faith produces works of gratitude and love.

Paul and James are at different points in the Christian life. Paul is at the beginning, and James is at some point after the beginning. Paul deals with the commencement of the Christian life and the initial experience of justification. He insists that no one can ever earn or win God's forgiveness; no one can put himself into a right relationship with God. That initial step must come from God's free and sovereign grace. It cannot be earned by obedience to God's Law, for the more a man strives to obey that Law the more he is convicted that he is a transgressor. He must come to God, therefore, "with nothing in his hands."

James begins later in Christian experience. He has in mind the professing Christian, the man who already claims to have been forgiven and to have entered into a right relationship with God so that he is justified through faith in the Lord Jesus. If this is so, as part of God's new creation (1:18) he must live a new life. Having been justified he must show that this is true by his progress in sanctification. Paul would have been in perfect agreement with James in this emphasis. Writing to Christians, Paul stresses that faith works or expresses "itself through love" (Gal. 5:6). Although we are not saved *by* works we are saved *for* them: "For we are God's workmanship, created in Christ Jesus to do good works, which God prepared in advance for us to do" (Eph. 2:10).

Paul aims at disillusioning those who think that

they can rest in their own good works in place of faith in the Lord Jesus. James aims at disillusioning those who think that just to profess faith in the Lord Jesus, without the active obedience of good works, is sufficient. They are dealing with different situations and what they say is entirely complementary.

We can perhaps see the perfectly complementary nature of these two emphases in the actual experience of Abraham. James mentions God's declaration of Abraham's justification (2:23) as well as Abraham's act in offering up his son Isaac (2:21). Now from the book of Genesis we know that a large number of years separated the two events, and that God declared Abraham righteous on account of his faith (Gen. 15:6) long before the time of God's call to him to be prepared to sacrifice his son (Gen. 22:2). Abraham's justification was by faith, and by faith alone—Paul's emphasis. But the proof of that justification was seen in the obedient life Abraham lived, and years later in his offering of Isaac—James's emphasis.

If we ask ourselves two questions, "Are there people who believe that their good works merit them salvation?" and "Are there professing Christians whose lives show no evidence of living faith?" we soon see how relevant are the two emphases Paul and James so effectively present.

In the second proof James turns from the most obvious example of Abraham to choose perhaps the least obvious! *Rahab* was a disreputable woman. The Bible makes no bones about it—she was a prostitute. She was a Canaanite who lived in Jericho. Prior to the conquest of the city, Joshua sent two men to spy out the situation in the city. Rahab not only gave them shelter but also saved their lives. The reason for her action is declared in Hebrews 11:31: "By *faith* the prostitute Rahab, because she welcomed the spies, was not killed with those who were disobedient." In the Joshua narrative Rahab declared her faith, "The Lord your God is God in heaven above and on the earth below" (Josh. 2:11). But the reality of Rahab's faith—which is James's point—was displayed in her works in that she protected the spies at risk to her own life. *Faith* was the moving cause of her *action*. She was "considered righteous for what she did when she gave lodging to the spies and sent them off in a different direction" (Jas. 2:25). In using Rahab as well as Abraham, James illustrates how universal is the nature of the principle he has put forth: it does not matter who it is—Jew or Gentile—the proof of justifying faith is in deeds, in righteousness and obedience.

Q.E.D.

Q.E.D. are the initials placed at the end of a mathematical conclusion that is beyond dispute, and that is something of the nature of James's statement in verse 26: "As the body without the spirit is dead, so faith without deeds is dead."

We may describe a body as a body whether it has a spirit in it or not. In the same way a person may be described by some as a believing man because he says he is. But we all know that while a body without a spirit is still a body, it is also a dead body—it is a corpse which needs to be disposed of quickly. So too, faith without works is dead. A professing of faith without works and the obedience of faith is as useless as a dead body, and as offensive too if nothing is done about it. James could not put the truth more plainly!

To test whether or not a body has life, we may place a thin piece of paper to the body's nostrils or lips, and if there is no perceptible movement, we may reasonably assume that no life exists and the body is dead. To test whether or not our profession of faith is genuine, we must put the New Testament's clear requirements of obedience and works of faith up against our life. If there is no perceptible correlation we must conclude that our faith, no matter how strongly affirmed in word, is, in fact, dead.

Make a list of what you would regard as some of the most obvious works of faith and try, where possible, to put them in some order of priority.

Compare James 2:24 with 2 Peter 1:10. In what ways do these verses explain each other?

What other Old Testament characters could James have used in addition to Abraham and Rahab to illustrate the relationship between faith and works? (Check your list afterwards with Hebrews 11.)

Seven

THE TONGUE
James 3:1-12

Warning people of danger is not an attractive activity, but it is a vital part of the Christian teacher's function (see Col. 1:28).

A Warning Against Danger

This chapter begins with a caution, the essence of which is the fact that *responsibility brings accountability*. Our Lord put it in a nutshell when He said, "From everyone who has been given much, much will be demanded" (Luke 12:48). James cautions his readers not to be presumptuous in taking upon themselves the function and task of a teacher (3:1). In many spheres of life presumption is a danger, but James spotlights particularly the teaching function.

He may be dealing with a particular pastoral problem of which we have no details. The teacher is a public figure. Of necessity, and not necessarily of choice, he is in the public eye. His prominence can be a seeming advantage that some people foolishly covet. The desire to be well known, well thought of or prominent, can therefore cause individuals to want the privilege of teaching others—but for these wrong reasons.

Many Jewish parents' ambition was to have their sons trained as rabbis or teachers, and it may be that some Jewish Christians carried over this kind of ideal into their Christian faith.

The church of Jesus Christ always requires teachers (1 Cor. 12:28,29; Eph. 4:11), but only so many in proportion to the other gifts of the Holy Spirit to the Body of Christ. The church is like the human body in its variety of functions and gifts, but it is not *all* tongue—in fact, far from it!

Teachers were recognized by the early church as of great importance, probably third in order of prominence (1 Cor. 12:28). Whenever they are mentioned, they are mentioned with honor (Acts 13:1; 1 Cor. 12:28; Eph. 4:11). The apostles and early missionaries were always on the move, not staying for too long a period in any one area. Teachers, however, worked usually within one fellowship or church. Their responsibility was to build converts up in the faith, and to show the way forward to Christian maturity in Christ. Their obvious importance in the life of the local church may have caused some immature Christians to covet the teacher's task.

James may be making this observation because, as he writes this letter, he finds himself appreciating afresh the tremendous responsibility he himself exercises as a teacher in writing to God's people in this way. Notice that little phrase in verse 1 "*we who teach.*" James applies what he says to himself. There are times when any teacher, genuinely called of God, will feel, "What a dreadful responsibility I have! How frightful if I say the wrong things and lead people astray! Who is sufficient for such great responsibility!" Like James, pastors and others have the function of teachers (Eph. 4:11), and they should regularly recall that their lives will be carefully examined by God to see how they have themselves fulfilled what they have instructed others to be and do.

James may simply be amplifying his exhortation of chapter 1, verse 19: "My dear brothers, take note of this: Everyone should be quick to listen, slow to speak and slow to become angry." It is entirely appropriate that Christians should "teach and admonish one another" (Col. 3:16) but with the qualification Paul made that it should be "with all wisdom." Christians in most, if not all, periods of history have been known to take the first part of the apostle Paul's exhortation to the point where they have sadly ended up censoring and reproving others where it has not been appropriate for them to do so. The desire to teach must not have behind it the desire to put others in their place. Censuring and reproving are part of the teaching ministry but they must never be enjoyed or revelled in by those whose responsibilities oblige them to engage in them.

One of the qualifications for a true teacher is his ability to give rebuke. "Do not rebuke a mocker or he will hate you," says the writer of Proverbs; "rebuke a wise man and he will love you. Instruct a wise man and he will be wiser still; teach a righteous man and he will add to his learning" (9:8,9). Our own willingness to accept deserved rebuke—our basic teachableness—influences our ability to help and instruct others.

Whatever his motive, James underlines the responsibility of a teacher's position: "We who teach will be judged more strictly" (3:1). Privilege equals responsibility, and responsibility brings accountability. "We must all appear before the judgment seat of Christ, that each one may receive what is due him for the things done while in the body, whether good or bad" (2 Cor. 5:10).

Our Lord Jesus Christ gave similar warnings. "Do

not judge," He said, "or you too will be judged. For in the same way you judge others, you will be judged, and with the measure you use, it will be measured to you" (Matt. 7:2). The danger for the teacher is that in applying the Word of God to the lives of others he may be harsh with them in a way he is not harsh with his own sins. Our Lord went on to speak of this danger, "Why do you look at the speck of sawdust in your brother's eye and pay no attention to the plank in your own eye? How can you say to your brother, 'Let me take the speck out of your eye,' when all the time there is a plank in your own eye? You hypocrite, first take the plank out of your own eye, and then you will see clearly to remove the speck from your brother's eye" (Matt. 7:3-5). The teacher is much more vulnerable than others to making this mistake (see Mark 12:38-40).

In passing, it is worthwhile noting that instruction was given to the early Christians about the judgment to come, and it was something in the light of which they were encouraged to live. James is able to write, "Because *you know* that we who teach will be judged more strictly" (3:1).

James backs up the seriousness of this reminder of the judgment by emphasizing the sad ease with which we may sin by our words. We all make mistakes in many ways, but in none more easily than by our words. Sin is likened to stumbling (3:2), as before (2:10). We may not choose to fall into this peril, but it may suddenly come upon us like a man tripping over a stone. And, if we are honest with ourselves, we are all guilty for "if anyone is never at fault in what he says, he is a perfect man, able to keep his whole body in check" (3:2). Our Lord used this word *perfect* when He urged, "Be perfect, therefore, as your heavenly Father is perfect" (Matt. 5:48), and also when He said to the rich young man, "If you want to be perfect, go, sell your possessions and give to the poor, and you will have treasure in heaven. Then come, follow me" (Matt. 19:21). God is perfect, and part of His perfection is that He never says a word out of place, and all His words are good. Anything short of God's pattern and example is sin.

The danger inherent in any exercise of the teaching ministry in the church of Jesus Christ is that it involves the use of speech, and that is the area of life in which we all sin most readily. "He who guards his mouth and his tongue keeps himself from calamity" (Prov. 21:23), but such an exercise does not come easily to us. Alexander Whyte exercised a most influential ministry in Edinburgh, and he wrote in a letter, "No man living has more woe than I have at myself because of my unadvised and offending words. And, however often I keep silent, and however much I prepare myself before I speak, my feet will sometimes go so far from under me that I suffer some sore falls, and am an offence to my best and most patient friends."

The Tongue's Capacity for Mischief

James's caution regarding rushing into a teacher's position, on account of the perils it may bring in the use of the tongue, leads him naturally to point out the tongue's evil potential (3:3-6).

We may be misled by the tongue's smallness (3:5). It is one of the smaller members of the human body—it is not as large, for example, as either a hand or a foot. But we should not judge the tongue's potential for influence by its smallness. Small things in many spheres may accomplish far more than larger objects.

James employs two illustrations. First, we put a bit into a horse's mouth in order to control it (3:3). The bit, however, is the smallest fraction of the horse's total size; yet it can be used to turn the whole animal without difficulty. Second, we use a rudder to steer a ship (3:4). The pilot knows the direction in which he wants the ship to go and he determines his course by a very small rudder. If the ship is large, the rudder still remains small in comparison. Even when the winds are strong and contrary to the ship's direction, the rudder continues to hold the ship on its determined course. The human tongue is like both the bit and the rudder in its smallness, and it far surpasses them in its power to influence, direct and sway the course of men's lives. It is capable of tremendous achievement.

The tongue "makes great boasts" (3:5). In one sense, the tongue's boasts are legitimately great in that it can produce evidence from history and contemporary life of what it has achieved. Men and women have been inspired to great endeavors as their leaders have exercised their eloquence to move them into action. In another sense, the tongue's boasting is a tragedy, for we may use our tongues to express our arrogance and self-confidence, and to declare our independence of God.

While the tongue has the power to do good, it can do irreparable harm. It can do in human life what a spark does to a forest—it can set it completely on fire (3:5). In most forests signs indicate the seriousness of accident through fire. Forest fires are frightening in their speed and devastating fury. Once words have been spoken they cannot be retracted, and they may spark off such fires of anger and hurt that people never recover from them (3:6).

The tongue is a "world of evil among the parts of the body" (3:6), by which James seems to mean that every sort of evil found in the world finds an ally in an uncontrolled tongue. As we ponder this statement we discover how profound a truth it is. Evil suppresses truth (Rom. 1:18), but men use their tongues in threats and other pressures to stop truth being known. Evil rejoices in evil and can make jokes about it (1 Cor. 13:6), and men use their tongues to express their pleasure in wrong things. Evil deceives and thinks nothing of giving a false impression (2 Thess. 2:10) and men use their tongues to deceive. In fact, the tongue "corrupts the whole person" (3:6). If we *speak* evil, we soon *do* evil. If we are bold enough to talk of sin, we'll soon be sufficiently bold to commit it. The order is *thought, speech* and *action*. To declare that what we say is only talk amounts to self-deception. The tongue can set the whole course of our life on fire (3:6) in that its misuse can spoil every good relationship and lead to the destruction of the things we would really hold to be the most precious. Marriages and good family relationships have been ruined by the tongue. Churches have been split and irreparably damaged in their witness by the ferocity of uncontrolled tongues.

The sad truth about the tongue's evil potential is that it "is itself set on fire by hell" (3:6). Hell or *Gehenna* originally denoted the valley of the sons of Hinnon, a ravine south of Jerusalem. There, according to later Jewish popular belief, the last judgment was to take place. In the Gospels it is the place of punishment in the next life (Matt. 23:33), the fiery destination to which the ungodly will be eternally condemned at the last judgment (Matt. 5:22; 18:9). Since hell is God's judgment upon Satan, to be set on fire by hell is synonymous with being under the influence of Satan and due to share in his destiny. Our Saviour spoke more of hell than He did of heaven, and we are compelled to face up to its awful reality. Our response to the tongue's evil potential may be, "Well, let's do something about it!" But that is easier said than done!

The Untameable Nature of the Tongue

It is true that most wild and potentially harmful creatures can be tamed by men expert in the task.

"All kinds of animals, birds, reptiles and creatures of the sea are being tamed and have been tamed by man" (Jas 3:7). When God blessed male and female at the creation, He said, "Be fruitful and increase in number; fill the earth and *subdue* it. *Rule over* the fish of the sea and the birds of the air and over every living creature that moves on the ground" (Gen. 1:28). When God made His covenant with Noah, He promised, "The fear and dread of you will fall upon all the beasts of the earth and all the birds of the air, upon every creature that moves along the ground, and upon all the fish of the sea; they are given into your hands" (Gen. 9:2; see also Ps. 8:6-8). We have but to visit either the circus or the zoo to confirm James's observation in the light of God's creation promise.

But the tongue is a different matter altogether! While man may proudly think he can tame anything, he cannot tame his own tongue. Man's tongue is "a restless evil" (Jas. 3:8). Evil, like its author, is restless (see Job 1:7; 2:2), and restlessness marks man's uncontrolled tongue. It is never sufficiently at rest to be brought under control. Worse still, it is "full of deadly poison" (Jas 3:8). James reflects many Old Testament statements here about the tongue, as, for example, when the psalmist describes evil men's devising of evil plans: "They make their tongues as sharp as a serpent's; the poison of vipers is on their lips" (Ps. 140:3). How many good relationships have been poisoned and even killed by the uncontrolled use of the tongue! (We ought to note, in passing, that while the tongue is untameable by man, it is not untameable by God: the fruit of the Spirit has self-control as an essential part of its manifestation. But God's control of our tongue is not James's subject.)

The Tongue's Relationship to the Heart
The challenging application of what James says

about the tongue is that we are made to appreciate the relationship of the exercise of our tongue and the spiritual condition of our inner man—what the Bible calls "our heart."

James points out the contradictory nature of much of our speech. One moment it is possible for us to use our tongues to praise God, our Lord and Father (3:9). That is of course one of the best and highest uses of our tongue and powers of speech. "O Lord, open my lips," we rightly cry, "and my mouth will declare your praise" (Ps. 51:15). But the tragedy is that it is possible for us in the next moment to curse men, men "who have been made in God's likeness" (Jas. 3:9), so that out of one and the same mouth there may come praise and cursing (3:10). John Bunyan, in his famous *Pilgrim's Progress*, describes Talkative in the following terms: "He was a saint abroad and a devil at home." When this state of affairs exists in any measure, all is not well. And James declares, "My brothers, this should not be" (3:10). Common sense tells us that something is wrong.

Once more James employs two illustrations from nature (3:11,12). Fresh water and salt water cannot flow from the same spring. James puts this truth in the form of a rhetorical question because he wants to carry his readers along with him in his argument. Fruit trees bear their own fruit and not that of another (3:12). If this pattern ceased to operate, we would know instantly that something was wrong. Similarly, true praise of God and cursing men do not flow from the same source, and they do not properly grow together. The problem then must be with our hearts—that is the implication of what James says.

James reflects here, as in many other places in his letter, the teaching of our Lord Jesus, and especially the Sermon on the Mount. Using the identical picture of a fruit tree, the Lord Jesus said, "No good tree

bears bad fruit, nor does a bad tree bear good fruit.
Each tree is recognized by its own fruit. People do not
pick figs from thornbushes, or grapes from briers.
The good man brings good things out of the good
stored up in his heart, and the evil man brings evil
things out of the evil stored up in his heart." Our
Lord's final comment is what we may describe as the
"punch line," the statement that brings conviction:
"For out of the overflow of his heart his mouth
speaks" (Luke 6:43-45). Elsewhere our Saviour
taught, "What comes out of a man is what makes him
'unclean.' For from within, out of men's hearts, come
evil thoughts, sexual immorality, theft, murder,
adultery, greed, malice, deceit, lewdness, envy, slander, arrogance and folly. All these evils come from
inside and make a man 'unclean' " (Mark 7:20-23).

What our tongue says is more than matched by
what our heart thinks. The tongue's relationship to
our heart is plain and uncomfortable. When our
tongues sin they display the depravity of our hearts
from which they speak. The overflow of our tongue is
the overflow of our heart.

James has already established that faith is proved
to be genuine by our works (2:14-26). Faith is also
proved to be genuine by our words, for words are part
and parcel of our works—we cannot separate what we
do from what we say. We actually *do* things to people—whether good or bad—by the way we speak to
them. The tongue may be used to make a true profession of faith (Rom. 10:6-9); but its wrongful use may
provide an evidence of a false profession of faith (Jas.
3:9). James emphasizes what he has already
expressed succinctly in 1:26: "If anyone considers
himself religious and yet does not keep a tight rein on
his tongue, he deceives himself and his religion is
worthless."

When our hearts are cleansed and put right with
God so that the Lord Jesus dwells in our hearts by

faith and reigns there by His Spirit, our words are brought under a new control (Gal. 5:22,23; see also Jas. 3:17,18). Only then dare we presume to exhort and teach others, whether in the one-to-one relationship of believer to believer, or in the public office of teacher if that is our calling. But even so, we must always guard our hearts. If we take care of our heart, the control of our tongue will take care of itself.

Read Mark 7:20-23. Which of the evils our Lord Jesus mentioned can find expression by means of the tongue?

What is the importance of spiritual teachers in the church, and what are the necessary qualifications for exercising the teaching ministry? (Are any aspects of 1 Timothy 3:1-7 reflected in James 3:1-12?)

In what ways in everyday life can the tongue be like a fire in its destructiveness? What safeguards can we impose upon ourselves to avoid its perils? (Consider as starters James 1:19; Col. 4:6.)

Eight

TWO WISDOMS
James 3:13-18

There is something that probably puzzles all of us at times. Why is there so much disorder and wrong in the most precious relationships we possess? A home should be the happiest of places, and yet it can be ruined by discord. The local church should be a picture of heaven's harmony, but it can be a place where disharmony is rampant. In the places we would expect to find peace and right relationships we may instead discover "disorder and every evil practice." James's answer is that there are two wisdoms, and they produce entirely different patterns of conduct. These two wisdoms are simply a reflection or outworking of the two great forces in the world, forces which may be expressed in a variety of ways: God and Satan, Light and Darkness, Truth and Error. If we possess the right wisdom, we shall solve most—if not all—of the problems that threaten our homes, our churches, and all our other relationships. James's subject, therefore, is of the utmost relevance to all.

The Existence of Two Wisdoms

The fact that there are two sorts of wisdom is a common theme in the Bible. The Old Testament contains what we know as "wisdom literature." The book of Proverbs is the most obvious example, and it is full of short, pithy sayings which lay down principles of personal happiness and well-being. There are other books—like Ecclesiastes and Job—which attempt to deal with man's basic questionings about the meaning of life and the relationship man should have with God.

When the book of Proverbs speaks of wisdom, it is not a theoretical or "classroom" wisdom, but wisdom for life. It wants to lead us into successful living. The revelation God gives us in His Word is a whole, and what the writer of Proverbs says about wisdom is completely consistent with what we find in the New Testament. For example, wisdom is available for any who will *seek* it (Prov. 1:20-23; Matt. 7:7,8). It comes by *revelation* (Prov. 2:6; Matt. 16:17; Luke 10:21), and it demands *a turning from evil* (Prov. 9:10; 8:13; Mark 1:15) and *obedience to the truth* (Prov. 8:34; Matt. 7:21,24). Wisdom requires *discipleship* (Prov. 2:1-5; Mark 1:17; Matt. 11:28-30).

The uniform testimony of the Bible is that God delights to give wisdom when it is sincerely and genuinely sought. Centuries ago "the Lord appeared to Solomon during the night in a dream, and God said, 'Ask for whatever you want me to give you.' " While Solomon could have asked for long life, wealth or the death of his enemies, he asked, instead, for wisdom. "Now, O Lord my God," he said, "you have made your servant king in place of my father David. But I am only a little child and do not know how to carry out my duties. Your servant is here among the people you have chosen, a great people, too numerous to count or number. So give your servant a discerning heart to govern your people and to distinguish between right and wrong. For who is able to govern this great people of yours?" (1 Kings 3:5,7-9).

The writer of Kings records, "The Lord was pleased that Solomon had asked for this" (3:10), and "God gave Solomon wisdom and very great insight, and a breadth of understanding as measureless as the sand of the seashore. Solomon's wisdom was greater than the wisdom of all the men of the East, and greater than all the wisdom of Egypt. He was wiser than any other man, including Ethan the Ezrahite—wiser than Heman, Calcol and Darda, the sons of Mahol. And his fame spread to all the surrounding nations. He spoke three thousand proverbs and his songs numbered a thousand and five" (1 Kings 4:29-32). It is wisdom of this character that we require in order to live our lives successfully.

The Wisdom of the World

First, however, there is what we may describe as the wisdom of the world. We employ the word *world* here in the sense in which it is used in the fourth verse of the next chapter. *World* is used sometimes simply to describe the world in a geographical sense (John 1:10), or the men and women of the world (John 3:16,17). Most frequently, it refers to the life of men and women as dominated and organized by the god of this world, Satan (2 Cor. 4:4; 1 John 2:15-17), and that's the sense we now have in view. The world tries to impress upon us its own kind of wisdom. John Bunyan summed it up in his description of Mr. Worldly Wiseman in *Pilgrim's Progress*. Mr. Worldly Wiseman's counsel was subtle in that he recommended Christian to get rid of his burden, but not by means of the Cross. He condemned the counsel that good Evangelist had given to Christian, and poured scorn on men who take the Bible—God's wisdom—seriously.

James provides a threefold description of worldly

wisdom, a wisdom which leaves God out of its reckoning.

First, this wisdom is "earthly" (Jas. 3:15). Literally, it is "on the earth" in contrast to that which is from heaven (see 1 Cor. 15:40; 2 Cor. 5:1; Phil. 3:19,20). It finds its origins in the earth rather than in heaven. It does not rise beyond the horizons of this world in its thinking or aspirations. All success is measured by achievement in this world.

Second, this wisdom is "unspiritual" (Jas. 3:15). It lives on the purely material plane without being touched by the Spirit of God (1 Cor. 2:14). It has in focus not the spiritual well-being of a man, but his material well-being. It does not encourage him to think of his soul but of his body and its pleasures. It fixes its attention not on spiritual treasure in heaven but on material possessions on earth. It is completely contrary in its reasoning to the way in which the Holy Spirit would lead the twice-born man (Jas. 1:18) to think and act.

Third, this wisdom is "of the devil" (3:15). It is demonic in origin. It finds its source with the evil powers of darkness; and Satan, their head, gives it every encouragement. When men and women follow the course this wisdom dictates they eventually find themselves with the devil in hell.

The Wisdom that Is from Heaven
Happily, there is on the other hand, the wisdom that is from heaven (3:17). *Heaven* is an equivalent word for *God*. The Jews had such a profound respect for God's name that they refrained from uttering it where possible and used replacement words. For example, when the prodigal son sought to express his repentance to his father, he spoke of having sinned "against *heaven* and against you" (Luke 15:21). James has talked already about God's wisdom in chapter 1 (1:5). God delights to give wisdom in

answer to requests for it. But behind these requests there must be genuine faith in Him and in His willingness and ability to grant it. He gives His wisdom not to the double-minded, but to the single-minded (1:8). Solomon, to whose example we have already referred, asked with single-mindedness and was not disappointed.

Two Sorts of Behavior

Heart and life go together—as we have said earlier. Mind and behavior are married. The existence of two sorts of wisdom inevitably brings about two sorts of behavior. James's consistent concern is with conduct, with our way of life (3:13). He underlines again the truth that a life cannot be separated from deeds. "Who is wise and understanding among you?" he asks. "Let him show it by his good life" (3:13). Conduct provides the best proof of wisdom even as it does of faith.

The wisdom that is in opposition to God's wisdom produces easily identifiable characteristics and behavior. It often contains the element of *bitterness* (3:14). Bitterness can be like a root that grows up in a person's life and poisons his whole attitude and character (Heb. 12:15), a fact which may be more obvious to others than to the person himself. Bitterness displays itself in attitudes of animosity, anger, and harshness. Anyone who differs with the views of the person with bitterness in his heart soon becomes an opponent, and even an enemy to be gotten rid of.

Envy and bitterness go together (Jas. 3:14-16). Envy is really zeal which has become twisted and has gone wrong. Out of feelings of bitterness, it is possible to be zealous for a cause or a course of action not because it is obviously one hundred percent right, but because it opposes a person or people against whom bitterness is felt. "Bitter envy" may be "harbored" in the heart without anyone else knowing about it, but a crisis may bring it to light with devastating effect.

Selfish ambition (3:16) gives rise to strife and contentiousness. Before New Testament times this particular Greek word was used only in Aristotle where it denotes a self-seeking pursuit of political office by any means, fair or unfair. James and John, the sons of Zebedee, were displaying something of this spirit when they went to the Lord Jesus and having asked, "We want you to do for us whatever we ask," they went on to request, "Let one of us sit at your right and the other at your left in your glory" (Mark 10:37). The desire behind the request came not from God but from the world, and was proof of a worldly spirit (1 John 2:15-17; Jas. 4:4).

To allow ourselves to be guided in our behavior by the wisdom of the world sets our feet on a slippery slope. Evil behavior escalates the more we allow it to become habitual. James indicates some of the disastrous consequences of living solely according to the wisdom of this world.

First, there is often boasting (3:14). Men may be so gripped by bitterness, envy and selfish ambition, that they even boast about things of which they should be ashamed.

Second, the false wisdom of this world may lead a person to lie against the truth, to say things which he knows are untrue (3:14). False wisdom argues that it does not always pay to tell the whole truth, and that half-truths may be acceptable. But half-truths are often not truth at all but deception.

Third, there is disorder (3:16). When the other disciples heard of James's and John's selfishly ambitious request to Jesus for prominence in His kingdom, it is not surprising that they became angry and indignant (Mark 10:41). Worldly wisdom, both inside and outside the church of God, brings tumult, disturbance and unruliness. Instead of bringing people together in understanding, it divides them through misunderstanding.

Fourth, every evil practice follows (Jas 3:16). "One thing leads to another" is a commonplace saying, and evil demonstrates its truth. Behind all the divisions in politics—and then in the individual political parties themselves—and among Christian bodies, there is usually a story of envy and selfish ambition. The disorder and wrong things that have been permitted to happen are all traceable to reliance upon the wisdom of the world in preference to seeking and following God's wisdom. Evil behavior, unchecked, always escalates. We cannot stand still in character formation—we either go forward or backwards.

The character and behavior produced by God's wisdom are in complete contrast to the world's earthly and unspiritual wisdom. The wisdom God gives is always in parallel with *understanding* (Jas. 3:13; see also Deut. 1:13; 4:6; Dan. 5:11). That is another way of saying that it is not just intellectual knowledge, which so easily makes a man proud, but it is practical knowledge as to how to live successfully. It shows itself in a *good life* with an outflow, by implication, of good *deeds* (Jas. 3:13).

James spells out the good life which God's wisdom produces, a good life proved good by its good deeds. We may discern at least nine characteristics. Prominent, as the background to the rest, is *humility* (3:13). There is no surprise about this when we remember the remarkable example of the Lord of glory "in whom are hidden all the treasures of wisdom and knowledge" (Col. 2:3), who humbled Himself for our sakes (Phil. 2:7; see also John 13:1-17). The divine wisdom puts selfish ambition or vain conceit out of the question, and replaces such attitudes with the determination to consider others better than ourselves, and to see things from other people's point of view (Phil. 2:3,4).

Purity is a foremost characteristic of the wisdom God imparts (Jas. 3:17). It is not a mixture as human wisdom is. When we give advice, we may be influenced often by personal considerations and by what may be best in the other person's decision for our own convenience or profit. We may want to give good advice but it may be rendered impure by our impure motives. God's wisdom enables us to apply principles to our own lives, and sometimes—when called upon to do so—to the lives of others, with a wisdom that determines to be totally uninfluenced by personal considerations because of its unreserved commitment to truth.

Peace loving (3:17) is an excellent way to describe peaceableness. It is possible to be peaceable because there seems to be nothing to be gained from being the opposite. But to be peace loving is to be peaceable because we love peace and want to do all we can to promote it. God Himself is described as the God of peace (Phil. 4:9; 1 Thess. 5:23), and it is not surprising, therefore, that the wisdom He gives promotes peace.

The Greek word behind the *NIV* translation "considerate" in verse 17 is one of the most difficult Greek words to translate into English. *Considerateness* is what Matthew Arnold called "sweet reasonableness." It is the opposite of anything approaching violence and quarrelsomeness (1 Tim. 3:3). It is the characteristic of a man who is always fair and gracious in his judgments and reactions to others. He does not insist upon the letter of the law being fulfilled but rather the spirit. He is not petty in his dealings with others but generous.

Linked with considerateness is *submissiveness* (Jas. 3:17). The King James translation "easy to be intreated" conveys the truth that this submissiveness expresses itself in the willingness to listen and to be persuaded by good grounds of reasoning. It does not want to be stubborn but open to what is right and best. Probably we all know of situations where we have entered into a meeting, supposedly for discussion and the discovery of God's will, but we have been determined beforehand not to change our mind. The wisdom from above makes us open to proper persuasion on the grounds of truth.

Mercy (Jas. 3:17) is one of God's essential qualities (Rom. 15:9; 2 Tim. 1:2), and it is mirrored in the wisdom He gives. Mercy is the feeling aroused by contact with the difficulties or sufferings which have come upon others, especially when they are in some measure undeserved. It does not stop at feeling, however, but moves into helpful action on behalf of those in need. In practice it means being utterly faithful in attempting to meet the needs of others. James underlines this important feature of divine wisdom by describing it as being "full of mercy"; its proportions are always sufficiently ample to cover the needs with which it is faced. The wisdom that is from above does not stop at words when it sympathizes but it moves into action.

Good fruit (Jas. 3:17) sums up the good actions to which true wisdom leads. Fruit does not appear all at once, and it may take considerable time to mature, but once there it is a proof of the existence of the divine wisdom in a human life. The New Testament has no time for mere intellectual knowledge or wisdom: the wisdom God gives is wisdom for *living*—it makes a man a better man, and his works prove him to be a better man.

Impartiality and *sincerity* go together (Jas. 3:17). The word translated "impartial" carries the meaning of various words and phrases which may better express it. We have no one word in the English language which expresses the Greek word. "Without uncertainty" or "without wavering" expresses best the meaning. The wisdom God gives is neither wavering nor hesitant. When it makes a decision, it does not then begin to doubt whether the right decision has been taken. It knows its own mind and sticks by the decisions it makes.

Sincerity means genuineness and freedom from hypocrisy. It does not, for example, pretend to be certain and without doubts when the opposite is the case. What it says it means. What it professes it genuinely believes. Those who are filled with God's wisdom are never underhanded but they are utterly straightforward. (A proof that these are characteristics of "the wisdom that comes from heaven" is that our Lord Jesus, "the man from heaven" (1 Cor. 15:49), exhibited all of these delightful fruits of wisdom in His earthly life.)

Remarkable Parallels

The unity of Bible truth is a remarkable evidence of the inspiration of Scripture by the Holy Spirit. James's description of the two wisdoms parallels Paul's description of *the works of the flesh* and *the fruit of the Spirit* (see Gal. 5:19-21 and 5:22-23). The wisdom that is "earthly, unspiritual, of the devil" (Jas. 3:15) partners the works of the flesh (Gal. 5:19-21), and "the wisdom that comes from heaven" (Jas. 3:17) partners the fruit of the Spirit (Gal. 5:22-23).

Over the centuries Christians have recognized in the book of Proverbs that wisdom is described as a Person, and that often the only proper identification of that Person can be the Lord Jesus Christ, the second Person of the Trinity (see Prov. 8, and particularly verses 22 onwards). The fruit of the Spirit, if added up like an arithmetical sum, provides us with a picture of our Lord Jesus Christ's character. Since the fruit of the Spirit and the wisdom that is from above go so clearly together, the proper conclusion is that divine wisdom in a man is nothing less than the

Lord Jesus dwelling in him by the Holy Spirit. Both the fruit of the Spirit and the divine wisdom indwelling us are proof that Christ is in us, "the hope of glory" (Col. 1:27).

Since, as Christians, we are part of God's new creation (see Jas. 1:18) with the divine seed of God's Word implanted in our souls, the fruits of God's divine wisdom are intended to grow in us. And so they will if we are obedient to the Word of God as it continues to be taught and preached to us (1:22-25). As we are obedient to the Word of God, we shall produce "a harvest of righteousness" (3:18). The proof that God's wisdom rules in us rather than the world's wisdom is that we are consistently peacemakers. What is more, we "raise a harvest of righteousness" by the character of the Lord Jesus which we exhibit in our own character and dealings with others. And it is this spiritual harvest in our lives which really proves that we are part of God's spiritual harvest through His Son's redeeming work at Calvary (Jas. 1:18).

Two Sorts of Teachers

The context of this passage demands that we appreciate that there may, sadly, be two sorts of teachers. We must not forget that teachers have been James's theme in the earlier part of the chapter. Teachers use their tongues more than most, and it is by our tongues, more than anything else, that we show the kind of wisdom which predominates in our life.

Teachers reveal by their tongues what kind of wisdom they possess. Teachers show, therefore, by the kind of harvest they produce among God's people whether or not they are called by God. Self-appointed teachers, not called by God, will most probably not be bothered very much if what they teach is neither practiced by them nor exhibited in their own lives.

Their selfish motives may lead them to cause factions and disorder.

Genuine Christian teachers, however, called by God and filled with His Spirit, though not perfect, will be most concerned about their example ("good life" and "deeds" as in v. 13) and will sow in peace and produce a harvest of practical righteousness in men's and women's lives by means of their consistent teaching and example. While a faithful teacher's reward will be great (1 Pet. 5:4), great too will be God's judgment upon the unfaithful teacher, the man who insists on teaching without being called of God (Jas. 3:1).

A Challenge

To those who long for the task of a teacher—and God Himself puts a rightful longing into the hearts of some—James says, in effect, "Test your life first." "Who is wise and understanding among you? Let him *show* it by his good life, by deeds done in the humility that comes from wisdom" (3:13). Notice how unrelenting James is in his demand for *deeds*. Ringing no doubt in his ears, as ought to be the case in ours, are the words of our Lord Jesus, "Let your light shine before men, that they may see your good deeds and praise your Father in heaven" (Matt. 5:16). Praising God is what the Christian life is all about. When worldly wisdom governs either the individual Christian's life or the corporate life of God's people, God is not praised; rather He is dishonored by unworthy or disgraceful conduct. But when God's wisdom reigns, God is praised by His people and then by the world as it sees how wonderfully God's people live together in love and unity.

While but few are called to be teachers in the public ministry of God's Word, we are all called upon to be ready to "teach and admonish one another with all wisdom" (Col. 3:16) as occasion demands. We all need to ask ourselves, therefore, "Am I qualified to teach and counsel my fellow-believers? Which wisdom rules in my life?"

"No one ever spoke the way this man does" (John 7:46). In what ways did the Lord Jesus exemplify the wisdom described in James 3:17?

We do not and cannot deny the value of much human wisdom, and James does not do so. Rather he criticizes human wisdom when it ignores God and is dominated by envy and selfish ambition. Taking human wisdom at its best, what are basic differences of viewpoint of the two wisdoms?

In verse 18 James uses the words *sow* and *harvest*. What are the practical implications of the use of these words? What do they teach us about the nature of Christian growth and maturity?

Nine

RETURN TO THE LORD
James 4:1-10

Backsliding may be an old-fashioned term, but it is, unfortunately, still a contemporary experience. This important section of James's letter constitutes an appeal to some of his readers who need to return to the Lord. Now no pastor or teacher appeals to God's people to *return* unless they have in some way or other *departed* from the Lord.

I once joined with others on a mission board to talk with a missionary who had recently returned from her first term of service in South America, working in translation work among an Indian tribe. Just she and another girl had spent long periods away from the main base, and for months they had foregone the privilege of corporate worship with other Christians. Among the questions she was asked was this: "How have things fared with your spiritual life during the time in the tribe?" I'll never forget both the immediacy and the honesty of her answer: "The seeds of backsliding," she replied, "are always in the heart." Robert Robinson expressed the truth similarly in his hymn, "Come, Thou Fount": "Prone to wander, Lord, I feel it, Prone to leave the God I love."

The Backslider's Characteristics

If we cast our minds back to what James has said earlier in his letter, we see how he has hinted already at many of the backslider's characteristics. The backslider is marked by instability in the face of trials (Jas. 1:2-8). One moment he wants to do the right thing and the next moment he seeks an easy way out, and he loses all the blessing God would give him by means of his trials.

The backslider finds himself infected by the world's false values of wealth (1:9-11). He thinks as a man of the world does rather than as a man of God.

The backslider loses sight of the eternal reward which should fill his vision (1:12). Having lost his closeness to God, the things which fill his physical vision assume greater importance than the things which have previously filled his spiritual vision.

The backslider then blames his temptations on everyone except himself (1:13-15). He becomes touchy and sensitive at any suggestion that he is to blame for his spiritual decline.

The backslider listens but does not obey God's Word as it is taught and preached (1:19-25). He may still be quite a connoisseur of sermons and an arguer of theology but he ceases to be a doer of God's Word. The backslider soon begins to sin more and more with his tongue because it is no longer under the Holy Spirit's control (3:1-12), and his life is guided by the unfortunate wisdom of the world rather than the divine wisdom (3:13-18). What James has said up to this point in his letter has equal relevance to all Christians, but the subjects under discussion are all extremely telling for the backslider. James now directly challenges the backslider.

A good physician or surgeon learns to recognize

telltale signs of illness or malignity. Both "fights" and "quarrels" were common among some of James's readers. If we immediately say, "Can this possibly be true among Christians?" the answer, sadly, is "Yes, among backsliding or unspiritual Christians." James, like an accomplished diagnostician, recognized these fights and quarrels among Christians to be a sign of something else—inner conflict. These believers were abrasive and unkind to one another because they were not at peace either within or with themselves, and, as a consequence, they took it out on one another. If, for example, a boss comes into work one morning, slams the door, shouts at his secretary and is rude to his associates, someone may hazard the probably accurate guess, "He's had a row at home!" The conflict in the office is a spin-off of the conflict in the home.

"Desires that battle within" (4:11) are the trouble; that's the sensitive spot upon which James puts his diagnostic finger. Most of the problems of human relationships—the flare-ups and the explosions—arise not so much from bad circumstances but from our bad desires. The conflicts and turmoil we know within ourselves are often greater than the conflict we occasion outside ourselves. They stay with us and can always be under the surface, whereas the outward confrontations and difficulties may be more occasional.

The fights, disagreements and quarrels of daily life and personal relationships come from our "desires that battle within" us (4:1). We often want something and we "don't get it" (4:2). When our hearts are double-minded, and thus away from God, they soon become caught up with the seemingly splendid and attractive cravings and boastings of the world. We set our hearts on some thing or some person, and when we do not succeed we become more and more dissatisfied and inwardly restless. We may get to the point where we have antagonism and anger towards people (which in our Lord's analysis may equal murder—Matt. 5:21,22) and covet what they possess.

Uncontrolled anger, hatred and coveting may even lead to physical violence and, in the heat of the moment, murder itself. Behind most quarrels and fights there is usually jealousy in some form. The man who is always fighting and aggravating others often has a pretty wretched battle going on inside himself. If he's honest he doesn't like what he sees inside him, and no one likes much what they see on the outside! The backslider is full of contradictions.

The Backslider's Dangerous Position

When we backslide, we lose our easy access to God, the access of children to their father. While we feel we ought to pray—and perhaps we continue to go through the motions of prayer—we know that we can't really pray with sincerity (Jas. 4:2b).

We recognize that we ought to bring our desires before God, but we are afraid to do so because that would mean they would be properly sorted out. And we are not prepared for that to happen. At the same time, we may sometimes try to pray. But our motives are wrong. We pray for things that we want, or we pray when things we value are threatened, but our prayers are selfish—they begin with what *we* want rather than with what *God* may want. We want more, simply that we "may spend . . . on . . . pleasures" (4:3). We are caught up with "everything in the world—the cravings of sinful man, the lust of his eyes" and his pride in possessions and, because such things come "not from the Father but from the world" (1 John 2:16), they separate us from the Father. They completely ruin our fellowship with Him. While we may be His children, we are like sons and daughters "in a distant country" who need to come to our senses

(Luke 15:13,17).

"You adulterous people, don't you know that friendship with the world is hatred toward God?" James asks (4:4). That may seem fairly strong language, but the dreadful situation demands it. Behind this frank use of the word "adultery" is the truth that our relationship to God through our Lord Jesus Christ is unspeakably precious and is quite unique in the universe. As Christians, we have been "promised" to Christ as a bride is promised to her husband (2 Cor. 11:2). God Himself is called the husband of His people (Isa. 54:5). In and through our Lord Jesus Christ, our relationship to God could not be closer. Our basic commitment above every other relationship is to the Lord Jesus. We are to set Him apart in our hearts as Lord (1 Pet. 3:15), for He is the rightful Lord of the totality of our life—body, mind, heart and spirit. The tragedy and hatefulness of worldliness is that we give these rightful possessions of the Lord Jesus Christ to the world. And in so doing, we become "adulterous people."

We must not misunderstand what James means by "friendship with the world" (4:4). He is not for a moment suggesting that we should neither be friendly nor have friendships with unbelievers. James has in view the world in its spirit of opposition to God and its cultivation of those attitudes and activities which are contrary to God's will. It is a matter of choice. We have to make choices all the time, and we can't avoid them. Every day we have to choose in a variety of ways whether to identify with the spirit of the world, in its preoccupation with possessions and with the frequent abuse of God's gifts, or whether we are going to identify with the Spirit of our Lord Jesus Christ, who would always lead us in the direction of right and good. Identifying with the Spirit, we inevitably stand out in the world and are different from the spirit of the world.

Sadly, we may choose to ignore the promptings of God's Spirit towards holiness. We may choose to ignore what we have been taught from God's Word. We may choose to think that we know better than God—not that we would put that thought into words, but that's what our actions and decisions may say. And before we know where we are, we may find ourselves on the world's side rather than God's. The sobering truth is that such friendship with the world constitutes hatred towards God.

We need to weigh James's words well, for he did not write them lightly: "Anyone who chooses to be a friend of the world becomes an enemy of God" (4:4). As Demas made his way to Thessalonica, "because he loved this world" (2 Tim. 4:10), he was making a choice which constituted "hatred" towards God. As Ananias and Sapphira put their love of money before their love for God, they made a decision which added up to "hatred" towards God. "People who *want* [same verb as James uses for *chooses*] to get rich fall into temptation and a trap and into many foolish and harmful desires that plunge men into ruin and destruction. For the love of money is a root of all kinds of evil. Some people, eager for money, have wandered from the faith and pierced themselves with many griefs" (1 Tim. 6:9,10). The backslider finds it uncomfortable to take his position seriously.

God Will Not Ignore Backsliding

James is earnest in what he says, and one of the reasons is that he is arguing on the basis of what God has spoken in His Word. The references to spiritual adultery are based on statements in the Old Testament which speak of God's covenant with His people. If God's people fail to take their relationship with God seriously, God always takes it seriously.

But now James quotes Scripture without telling exactly which Scripture he has in mind. It is possible that he is putting various thoughts of Scripture together. But before looking at the Scripture truth he writes, we must notice the two words "without reason" (4:5). God never says anything without reason. What God says on any subject is final. His word is utterly reliable, and it is His Word, rather than our feelings or convictions, which must guide our reactions and decisions. These thoughts make all the more significant the words which James now writes.

James 4:5 is difficult to translate, and modern translations illustrate the difficulty. Probably the best translation is "God yearns jealously over the Spirit." The *NIV* footnote translation expresses the thought well: "God jealously longs for the spirit that he made to live in us." It seems right to take this to be a reference to God the Holy Spirit. The wonder of our new birth (1:18) is that we are born again of God's Spirit, and our bodies become His temples (1 Cor. 6:19). The possession of the Holy Spirit is such an inseparable part of being a Christian that Paul can write, "If anyone does not have the Spirit of Christ, he does not belong to Christ" (Rom. 8:9). God will not take the Holy Spirit from us—for, if He did, we should cease to be His. Furthermore, He has covenanted with His Son that as a consequence of Calvary every believer shall be marked out as God's possession by the Spirit's indwelling.

But that indwelling of the Holy Spirit puts a great responsibility upon us. Wherever we go and whatever we do we take the Holy Spirit with us—for we are His temples. (This staggering truth was the basis of one of Paul's arguments about the dreadfulness of any immorality permitted in the Christian's body—1 Cor. 6:18,19). When we behave contrary to God's will we grieve the Holy Spirit who always wants to confirm God's will to us and help us to walk in it. When God's Word is preached or brought to us in some other God-appointed way, and we refuse it, we quench the

Spirit who is behind every means of bringing home God's Word to us.

There's no more precious guest than the Holy Spirit, and backsliding and all its consequences hurt Him. God is jealous for the proper treatment of His Spirit, and it distresses Him when we treat the Spirit's indwelling as a matter of little significance. The seriousness of backsliding overwhelms us when we truly see it in this light. When we backslide, our instability, our false values, our failure to listen to God's Word properly and to obey it, our misuse of our tongue, and our false wisdom all grieve God's Spirit, and God is angry with us. When we appreciate this, conviction of sin wells up within us, and so, of course, it should. Fortunately James does not end with this solemnizing truth of God's jealousy for His Spirit.

God Gives More Grace

"But he gives us more grace" (Jas. 4:6)—these must be among the sweetest words of Scripture. They are brief, yet utterly comprehensive. Grace is God dealing with us in kindness in a way we could never deserve; it is God dealing with us in the light of His love shown at Calvary. One of the principal qualifications for receiving grace is the knowledge that we don't deserve it! Grace exactly suits the need, therefore, of those who have backslidden and grieved God's Spirit.

While all the giving is on God's side, He requires humility from us. James quotes Proverbs 3:34 when he declares, "God opposes the proud but gives grace to the humble" (4:6). All the time we are proud, God must resist any endeavor we make to return to Him. To return to Him, we must really mean what we say, and the pursuit of reality demands self-humbling. We may fool ourselves about our pride, but we cannot deceive God.

Pride exhibits itself in self-justification, so that when the Holy Spirit puts the spotlight on our error or sin we make excuses or we try to place the blame onto others. We may even try to blame God for the situations in which we've landed ourselves (see Jas. 1:13-18). Any refusal on our part to face up to the honest truth about our sins is basically an exhibition of pride. It is for our good that God resists us while we are proud, for no return to Him will be sustained if our pride is undealt with by Him.

But once we genuinely humble ourselves, the floodgates of God's grace open and His love embraces us in all its fullness. The turning point in the parable of the lost son was when "he came to his senses" and determined to say to his father, "Father, I have sinned against heaven and against you. I am no longer worthy to be called your son" (Luke 15:17-19). Humility does not happen without cost and hurt to us, and it does not occur in a moment. There are steps towards it, and it is these steps which prove its genuineness.

There is considerable similarity between James 4:6 and 10. They both have to do with humility: the first is a statement and the second is an instruction. The purpose of verses 7-9 is to get the backslider from the position of recognizing his need of self-humbling to the point where he accomplishes it.

Steps to Humility

There is an undoubted significance in the order of the instructions given in James 4:7-9; it is important, therefore, that the order should be observed, and the relationship of one instruction to the other noted. None of the steps must be left out. It is rather like a doctor's prescription to be made up by the pharmacist: in order to be effective each ingredient must be present in its proper proportion. These steps, if followed humbly in their order, are infallible in their success. These steps constitute God's ordained way back for the backslider to his right relationship with God.

The first step is to "submit yourselves, then, to God" *(4:7).* Submission is different from our simply telling God where we have gone wrong. The deceitfulness of our hearts would easily lead us to be lenient with ourselves or to avoid facing up to the real issues which have grieved God's Spirit. Submission is our allowing God to show us where we have gone wrong. Of course, to begin with, we confess the obvious sins of which there is no doubt. But there is a place also for silence, for quietly waiting upon God that, by the use of our conscience and the Scriptures, the Holy Spirit may put His finger upon those areas of our lives where sorting out is required. As we submit ourselves to God in this way, the Holy Spirit who, we must remember, indwells us will not leave us without His witness. He may have to be a painful witness sometimes, but His motives are similar to those of a caring surgeon or physician.

When we go as a patient to a physician or surgeon we may complain of a pain in a certain part of our body. As the doctor examines us, we may say, "That's not where the pain is, doctor." His reply may be, however, "You must submit yourself to my examination. Your pain may be a symptom of something else, and that's why my examination must be wider than just the area of immediate and obvious pain." So it is with us when we have backslidden: it is not enough for us to simply tell God where we know we have pained Him; we must be prepared for His Spirit's detailed examination and report.

The second step is to "resist the devil," James urges, "and he will flee from you" (4:7). This instruction is precisely what the backslider has failed to do. Now he must return to what is the Christian's constant duty. The devil is the great enemy of our souls, the opposer of all that is good and the encourager of all that is bad.

The implication of the place of this instruction in the order of the steps for the returning backslider is that any return to the Lord will be immediately resisted by the devil. As soon as I come to my senses regarding any backsliding in my life, and seek to put it right, the devil whispers his unique insinuations, such as, "Beware! If you submit yourself to God, you don't know what He may require of you. Why, you may have to apologize to someone and confess that you have been in the wrong!" Resist him—James urges! When we resist the devil he will flee from us, not because we are strong enough but because God sees to it that if we mean business Satan does not have the final word.

The third step is to exercise faith (4:8). Once again the order deserves attention here. So often the backslider may be told, "Well, pray about your situation and confess your sins." But, as many of us know, that does not always work, and it is by no means as easy as that. "Come near to God" is an invitation to pray, but it is not the first step in James's instructions, and we can see why. There is little point in praying for forgiveness if we have not faced up to the seriousness of our sin (4:5), or the folly of our stubborn pride (4:6). We cannot accomplish our return to God if we are unwilling to submit ourselves to God's judgment on our life, or to resist the devil (4:7). While it is always right to pray, prayer must be joined with action.

Prayer is coming near to God. Although as backsliders we may have maintained a form of prayer, we will have lost our experience of "coming near" to God, and the confidence that God "rewards those who earnestly seek him" (Heb. 11:6). We must come as we first came—by means of the cross. The blood of Jesus Christ which first brought us to God also cleanses us from our backsliding. The cross is the only place we can lay down the burden of the guilt we know as we ponder what we have done to God's Spirit, our heavenly guest, by our waywardness and disobedience. But *all* the burden can be removed there, and God *will* come near to us! He deals with us as individuals, and in His own unique way He assures us by His Spirit that He hears our prayer, accepts our confession, and receives us. Our heavenly Father is pictured in the lost son's father who, when he saw his son, "was filled with compassion for him; . . . ran to his son, threw his arms around him and kissed him" (Luke 15:20).

But the work of returning to the Lord is not yet complete. We shall have expressed to God our repentance in *words* as we have submitted ourselves to Him and drawn near to Him in the name and merits of our Lord Jesus Christ. *But, the fourth step, repentance is a matter of works too (Jas. 4:8,9).* Repentance involves a complete change-round, a turnabout in our life's direction. Wrong things must go. *First, we must wash our hands (4:8).* Our hands represent our actions. Whatever we do we tend to employ our hands. The things we have done which have been wrong must be confessed and completely renounced. *Second, we must purify our hearts (4:8).* The heart is primarily the place of the affections. When we backslide we have loved the wrong things and put the wrong people on the throne of our heart in place of the Lord Himself. Our wrongful affections must be confessed and our hearts cleansed and made the undisputed throne of our Lord Jesus. *Third, we must rid ourselves of our double-mindedness (4:8).* When we backslide, two minds have been at work in us. In one sense we have been committed neither to the world nor to the Lord; and on the other hand it might be said that we have tried to be committed to both. We have been like a man trying to walk two ways at once. With our eyes on the Cross and upon our indebtedness to our Saviour, we must now want our mind to be renewed (see Romans 12:1,2). The wrong things we thought nothing of, about which we perhaps laughed or joked, must be confessed, mourned and regretted, and where possible, put right.

We come then to James's final instruction to backsliders: "Humble yourselves before the Lord, and he will lift you up" (4:9). As we follow the earlier steps, we arrive at the point where God can really meet with us in His grace and lift us up. *But we must humble ourselves.* It is true that He has begun this restoring work and that He assists us, but He wants us to *choose* to complete it. In days gone by we chose to be friends of the world; now we must choose to be God's friends, if that is what we really want. Each earlier step will further the work of self-humbling. Primarily, it is a humility before the Lord Himself, but it will then show itself before others. Initially it may involve not a few apologies, and some restitution. But it will also involve a new experience of God's grace! The Lord Himself will lift us up. He will assure us of His forgiveness. He will give us joy in our fellowship with Him. He will lift us up to levels of fellowship and service we never thought possible. There's a world of difference between the man who lifts himself up and the man whom the Lord lifts up. We must make sure that we are the latter.

Consider the fights and quarrels which take place, sadly, among people who profess to be Christians. What desires are frequently behind them? What should our attitude be when others try to draw us into such conflicts?

How would you define worldliness? Having made your definition, check it with John's in 1 John

2:15,16. What are the most obvious temptations to worldliness in your own life?

"The seeds of backsliding are always in the heart." If this is the case, what are the best precautions to take against backsliding?

Ten

THAT RESTLESS EVIL
James 4:11-17

Taming the tongue—this was James's subject in
chapter 3, verses 1-12. Dealing with this important
matter led him into an exposition of the two sorts of
wisdom which the tongue can display. His outlining
of the disastrous wisdom which belongs to the earth
and to the devil led him then, in turn, to deal with the
whole subject of backsliding (4:1-10). Part of the
backslider's tragic situation is that he lives according
to the world's wisdom rather than God's. But James
returns now to the subject of the tongue—that "restless evil" as he has described it in 3:8.

The Tongue and Slander
"Brothers, do not slander one another" (4:11). The
same verb is used three times in verse 11: once it is
translated as "slander" and twice as to "speak
against." To slander is to speak against someone—
that is what it is at its simplest. It includes lots of
other unpleasant uses of the tongue such as gossip-
ing (Rom. 1:29; 2 Cor. 12:20), malicious talk (1 Tim.

6:4), saying things that ought not to be said at all (1 Tim. 5:13), false testimony (Deut. 5:20), the spreading of false reports (Exod. 23:1), and the unhelpful repeating of stories about wrongs or offenses (Prov. 17:9).

"The words of a gossip are like choice morsels; they go down to a man's inmost parts" (Prov. 26:22).

Gossip has a peculiar fascination to fallen human nature, and it soon degenerates into a pulling of others to pieces. William Tyndale translated it as "backbiting," a most expressive term. It may seem inconceivable that Christians should ever allow themselves to slander one another, or indeed to slander anyone. But we must not deceive ourselves.

James begins this exhortation with the word *"Brothers"* (4:11). When Paul wrote his second letter to the Corinthians, he had to write, unfortunately, "I am afraid that when I come I may not find you as I want you to be, and you may not find me as you want me to be. I fear that there may be quarreling, jealousy, outbursts of anger, factions, slander, gossip, arrogance and disorder" (2 Cor. 12:20). Whenever "the wisdom that comes from heaven" (Jas. 3:17) is forsaken, we'll find in its place the wisdom that "is earthly, unspiritual, of the devil" which brings in its wake "disorder and every evil practice" (3:15,16).

Slander is part of the deadly poison (3:8) with which the tongue can be filled. It is a poison because it so easily prejudices our minds.

The most serious poisons are those for which there are no known antidotes. Once released they pursue their frightening course relentlessly. Slander is rather like that. We may put some brakes upon its progress, but once uttered it will do its evil work no matter how justly and zealously it may be refuted. I remember reading something of the dreadful effects of slander in the life of David Livingstone, the famous missionary to Africa. To safeguard his wife from some of the hardships that were inevitable in the initial stages of his establishing a home for her with him, he left her in a secure place until he had prepared a home for her at Lake Nyassa. But people began to talk unkindly, suggesting that he and she did not get on well together, and that Mrs. Livingstone was not a help to her husband. Dr. Livingstone was so troubled by these insinuations that he sent for his wife. She came, only to become ill and die. What a dreadful responsibility rests upon those who release poison with their tongues!

When we hear something bad of another person, the instinctive reaction so often is to think, "There's no smoke without fire." And almost without thinking about it, seeds of suspicion are accepted into our minds about the person who has been slandered. Even as I write I recall hearing someone drop in conversation a rather unpleasant remark and insinuation about another person. I immediately repudiated it and said I was as sure as I could be that the suggestion about this other person was incorrect. And yet the dreadful thing is that when that particular person comes to my mind now I can still find my memory recalling the unpleasant thing that was said about him. Such is the pernicious effect of slander. Once slander has been spoken, it is virtually impossible to do anything about it. Even to try and undo the harm that has been done may only aggravate the situation by drawing attention afresh to the false statements that have been made.

A story is told of a Christian teacher of the sixteenth century who found himself faced one day by a woman who confessed herself to be a slanderer. "Do you frequently fall into this fault?" he inquired. "Yes, very often," she admitted. "Your fault," he said, "is great, but the mercy of God is still greater. Go to the nearest market and purchase a chicken, just killed, and still covered with feathers. You will then walk a certain distance, plucking the bird as you go along. When you've finished your walk, return to me here."

The woman went to the market, bought the chicken, and set out on the journey, plucking it as she went along, just as she had been instructed. In a short time she returned, anxious to relate how exactly she had done what she had been told, and to see what it all meant. "Ah," said her teacher, "you have been very faithful to the first part of my orders. Retrace your steps, and gather up *one by one all the feathers you have scattered.*" "But," explained the woman, "I cast them carelessly on every side; the wind carried them in every direction. How can I recover them?" "Well," he replied, "so it is with your words of slander; like the feathers, they have been scattered. Call them back if you can. Go, and sin no more."

Slander is something we are *not* to do. To slander is to imitate the evil one, whose name *diabolos* means "slanderer." We need to recognize that slander belongs to our old life and we need to be rid of it (Eph. 4:31; Jas. 1:21). It will not only hinder our spiritual growth but it will ruin any testimony we may possess to the saving power of our Lord Jesus Christ. It is impossible to be in a right relationship with God and at the same time to indulge in slander. The New Testament takes the matter so seriously that Christians are told not to have anything to do with a professing Christian who persists in slander (1 Cor. 5:11).

James's exhortation concerning slander needs to be applied not only to the Christian in his personal or one-to-one relationships but also to the corporate relationships Christians possess. One group of Christians can so easily slip into the snare of slandering another, especially if they are of a different denomination or have a varying emphasis on some secondary point of doctrine. One local church can slander another. We need to be on our guard whenever the question is asked, "Have you heard what is going on at present at such and such a church?"

Charles Simeon, whose ministry in Cambridge was so influential, wrote a letter to a friend in July 1817 on how to cope with evil-speaking. The advice he gave was excellent and is as good a guide now as when it was first written.

"The longer I live, the more I feel the importance of adhering to the rules which I have laid down for myself in relation to such matters.

"1st   To hear as little as possible what is to the prejudice of others.

"2nd   To believe nothing of the kind till I am absolutely forced to it.

"3rd   Never to drink into the spirit of one who circulates an ill report.

"4th   Always to moderate, as far as I can, the unkindness which is expressed towards others.

"5th   Always to believe, that if the other side were heard, a very different account would be given of the matter."

The Tongue and Judging Others

"Anyone who speaks against his brother or judges him, speaks against the law and judges it" (Jas. 5:11). Slander and judging others are frequently linked. It is virtually impossible to speak against another person without falling into the trap of judging him. When we speak against someone—which is slander—we are usually saying that he has either done something wrong or that he has left undone something that he ought to have done. We may pass our remarks off as simply the expression of our opinion, but the truth is that we are passing judgment on another person—we actually judge him.

But in a proper court of law the judge strives to hear *all* the facts, and he also hears the accused's account of the facts. But when we slander others—

and thus in effect judge them—we never have *all* the facts. And we certainly don't have the accused persons in front of us to answer. In fact, we can never be totally reliable judges of others because we never see the whole situation as God does.

Once more James echoes our Lord's teaching in the Sermon on the Mount: "Do not judge, or you too will be judged. For in the same way you judge others, you will be judged, and with the measure you use, it will be measured to you. Why do you look at the speck of sawdust in your brother's eye and pay no attention to the plank in your own eye? How can you say to your brother, 'Let me take the speck out of your eye,' when all the time there is a plank in your own eye? You hypocrite, first take the plank out of your own eye, and then you will see clearly to remove the speck from your brother's eye" (Matt. 7:1-5). Our Lord's words remind us that the person who quickly judges others and speaks against them is the man who knows very little of himself and of his own sinfulness. The knowledge of our own failings makes us more and more hesitant about expressing any form of criticism of others. The man who knows himself learns an increasing silence before other people's faults.

The Bible is not without its own illustrations of the misjudging of others. One of the most exciting incidents in the Old Testament is the battle between David and Goliath. The story really began with Jesse, David's father, saying to David, "Take this ephah of roasted grain and these ten loaves of bread for your brothers and hurry to their camp. Take along these ten cheeses to the commander of their unit. See how your brothers are and bring back some assurance from them. They are with Saul and all the men of Israel in the Valley of Elah, fighting against the Philistines" (1 Sam. 17:17-19). And so it was that early in the morning David left his flock in the care of another shepherd, loaded up and set out in precise obedience to his father. When he arrived at the Israelites' camp he naturally enough inquired about the state of the battle. But then he was in for a big surprise. "When Eliab, David's oldest brother, heard him speaking with the men, he burned with anger at him and asked, 'Why have you come down here? And with whom did you leave those few sheep in the desert? I know how conceited you are and how wicked your heart is; you came down only to watch the battle' " (1 Sam. 17:28). Eliab completely misjudged David's motives for being there, he falsely accused him of abandoning his sheep to danger, and he uttered dreadful slanders against him. In the light of what James says about man's anger never bringing "about the righteous life that God desires" (Jas. 1:20), it is significant that 1 Samuel 17:28 describes Eliab as burning with anger.

James makes two further points we must note. First, when we speak against our brother or judge him, we speak against the law, and judge it (4:11). There are two ways of applying this truth. If I fall into the snare of judging someone, knowing full well beforehand that I ought not to do so, I am saying in effect that God's law—His royal law (2:8) which says that I must love my neighbor as myself—has no binding power on me and can be ignored. I act as if I judge God's law to be of no real consequence. To love my neighbor as myself must, at the very least, mean protecting his reputation as I would want my own to be protected. But if I judge my neighbor I'm saying that God's law can be ignored. And that is a most serious error.

The other way in which we speak against the law and even presume to judge it by engaging in slander or speaking against our brother is that we are saying, in effect, that we don't feel that we can wait for the law and the Judge to do their job. By our own words of judgment we imply that we need to anticipate the

Judge's action. By implication we are judging the Lawgiver as being either dilatory or inadequate; otherwise, why do we ourselves rush into judgment? For this reason James adds the comment, "When you judge the law, you are not keeping it, but sitting in judgment on it" (4:11).

When we judge others and speak against them, we are, if the truth is told, trying to push God off His judgment seat in order to place ourselves on it. This is an action of gross presumption because God's position is absolutely unique. First, He is the sole true Lawgiver (4:12). His laws alone are of permanent significance. Secondly, He is the one Judge of mankind (4:12). His judgments upon us are of eternal validity. He has the unique ability to both save and destroy. He says to us, "There is no god besides me. I put to death and I bring to life, I have wounded and I will heal, and no one can deliver from my hand" (Deut. 32:39). God alone is competent to judge justly (1 Cor. 4:4,5). For us to judge others, therefore, is to take upon ourselves a right which is God's. It is an infringement of God's prerogative. We do well to ask ourselves, "Who am I to judge my neighbor?" or as Paul asks, "Who are you to judge someone else's servant? To his own master he stands or falls" (Rom. 14:4). If we appreciate the presumptuousness of our judging others we'll tremble at the thought of engaging in it. We'll all find ourselves tempted to impatience with, and criticism of, other people's behavior at times, but it is a temptation we *must* overcome. Charles Simeon, whom we mentioned earlier, used to say, "Let us sit upon the seat of love instead of judgment."

The Tongue and Boasting About the Future

James moves on to another subject, but the tongue is still part of it. The tongue can be used to express an unjustified confidence about the future which is in conflict with a genuine confidence in God. "Now listen, you who say, 'Today or tomorrow we will go to this or that city, spend a year there, carry on business and make money' " (Jas. 4:13). The tongue can both *boast* and *brag* (4:16). It can boast in that by means of it we compare ourselves with others and we make sure that we come off best. It can brag in that we express big ideas about ourselves and exceed the bounds of reality.

The example James gives of the tongue's boasting is of businessmen, but we should not limit the application of what he says to them. The Jews have always been renowned as shrewd businessmen. James imagines businessmen sitting around their conference table making plans for future commercial enterprises (4:13). They were so sure of themselves that they spoke of what they would do, where they would go, and what profit they would make, without any restraint. They assumed that they could forecast what they were going to do on every day.

But their boasting tongues led them to overlook the fact of God's providence. God's providence is His good, kind and unceasing activity and control, so that He works out everything in agreement with the counsel and design of His own will. As we sometimes say, "Man proposes, but God disposes." It may sometimes appear that what men's tongues boast and brag about is justified when their plans all seem to work out smoothly. But, in fact, they do so only by God's permission.

The businessmen's boasting tongues led them to overlook their basic ignorance of what even the next day held (4:14): "Why, you do not even know what will happen tomorrow." "Do not boast about tomorrow," the writer of Proverbs urges, "for you do not know what a day may bring forth" (27:1). James backs up his caution by a question and a telling picture: "What is your life? You are a mist that appears for a little while and then vanishes" (4:14). (We ought to notice that James uses yet a further picture from nature.)

Elsewhere in the Bible similar pictures are used of the transitoriness of human life, such as the grass (Isa. 40:6), or the flower in the field (Job 14:2), a leaf before the wind (Job 13:25) and a shadow (Job 14:2). In many parts of the world we know what it is to wake up in the morning and to be aware of a mist. It all appears very permanent. But perhaps just a few moments later we may look out of our window again, and it's gone! The impermanence of the mist is a picture of the uncertainty and transitoriness of human existence. We seem to be settled and established, but suddenly our life may come to an end—and often without any warning. To make our plans without reference to God and to His control is really a form of practical atheism.

What we ought to be saying always as we make our plans is, "If it is the Lord's will, we will live and do this or that" (4:15). James is not suggesting that we pepper our conversation with liberal helpings of the phrase, "If it is the Lord's will" or that we put *D.V.*— the initials representing the Latin words *Deo volente* ("the Lord willing")—on all our invitations to meetings and special occasions. More important than the words or the initials is the conviction in our hearts that in all our plans we are dependent upon God and subject to His will. The psalmist was right when he wrote, "I trust in you, O Lord; I say, 'You are my God.' My times are in your hands" (Ps. 31:14,15). When the apostle Paul spoke of making visits to companies of believers "if the Lord is willing" (1 Cor. 4:19; 16:7), it was because he knew that his whole life needed to be mapped out by God if it was to be successful, and that he wanted God's control of his plans and movements.

When men boast and brag about their plans, their future successes and their prospects, they exhibit the world's wisdom; and their unbridled tongues, no matter how sophisticated the language, are "set on fire by hell" (Jas. 3:6).

The Tongue and Obedience

Throughout the whole of his letter James underlines the priority of obedience. It is not enough to know the truth; it must be obeyed. Knowledge without obedience constitutes dangerous knowledge because it increases our responsibility at the final judgment. He draws a conclusion now from what he has just been saying: "Anyone, then, who knows the good he ought to do and doesn't do it, sins" (4:17).

James probably recognizes that his letter has been read aloud up to this point to different congregations, and many will have been nodding their heads in agreement with what he has written. For example, early on in chapter 1, verse 19, he urged, "Everyone should be quick to listen, slow to speak, and slow to become angry." But a head nodding in agreement is no substitute for an obedient tongue! A practical outworking of the principle of 1:19 is the avoidance of the misuse of the tongue in slander, judging others and foolish boasting about the future, as described in this passage before us.

It is not enough to be a good hearer or reader in these matters, to be nodding our heads in agreement and then to do nothing. Knowledge and understanding of God's will are a stewardship. If a man doesn't know the right thing to do, he has some excuse for not doing it. But if he does know the right thing to do, and doesn't do it, there's no doubt at all about his guilt and sin. This observation that James makes is completely relevant to the subjects he has dealt with. If I ask myself, "Do I know slander is wrong? Do I appreciate that judging others is forbidden? Am I aware of the presumptuousness of boasting about the future?" I have to answer in the affirmative in each case. My duty, therefore, is plain: I must do *none* of these things.

Faith without works is dead (2:26). Hearing without obedience is useless. James 1:26 allows for no exceptions: "If *anyone* considers himself religious and yet does not keep a tight rein on his tongue, he deceives himself and his religion is worthless." Where there's living faith in God through our Lord Jesus Christ, and the obedience of faith, slander will be put to death, judging others will be banned, and boasting about the future will be replaced by quiet confidence in God's gracious control of our lives.

How real a problem in our church fellowship is unhelpful talking about other people? How may we deal with it positively and constructively when it arises?

How far is it right to make plans for the future? (Read, for example, Proverbs 6:6-8; and Joseph's instructions to Pharaoh in Genesis 41:28-40.) What considerations must govern all our plans if our trust is in God?

James 4:17 is one of the most challenging verses in the Bible about the nature of sin. It relates to what we sometimes call "sins of omission." Can you provide practical examples of good that you know that you ought to do but which you know you have failed to do?

Eleven

WEALTH, WAGES AND JUDGMENT
James 5:1-6

Warning to Rich Oppressors—that's how the *New International Version* describes this section of James's letter. It's an accurate description, but it immediately prompts questions. To whom is James addressing these severe words? To Christian congregations? Or to the world at large? The answer is that he is probably addressing both, and for different reasons.

His warning to rich oppressors provides an indirect encouragement to Christians who find themselves dismayed by the injustices of contemporary society. Many Christians throughout the world today ask, "How long will these injustices with which we have to live last? Why doesn't God bring them to an end?" The answer is that they will all end at God's judgment of the world, and they will all be put right.

James's warning is relevant too to double-minded Christians, to Christians who try to face two ways at once, whose allegiance is divided between God and the world.

But the absence of the word "brothers" at this point in James's letter (such as in 5:7,10,12) most likely indicates that James's words are directed principally at unbelievers.

Oppression is no new problem. The writer of Ecclesiastes urged, "If you see the poor oppressed in a district, and justice and rights denied, do not be surprised at such things; for one official is eyed by a higher one, and over them both are others higher still. The increase from the land is taken by all; the king himself profits from the fields" (5:8,9).

James's message is a burst of righteous indignation reminiscent of the Old Testament prophets. We must not forget, as we have mentioned earlier, that the kind of society in which James's readers lived was one where you were either very rich or very poor. We must not forget too that James's overall concern is with the relationship of faith to works. If a man possesses living faith in the Lord Jesus Christ and is materially wealthy, his faith will be seen in the worthwhile manner in which he uses his wealth. There are three strands of thought in this passage which we may separate for the convenience of our consideration: wealth, wages and judgment.

Wealth

Nowhere is it suggested in the Bible that it is wrong to possess wealth.

One of the proofs that James is not against riches or wealth as such is that he rightly commends Job later in the chapter (5:11), and Job was an extremely wealthy man, but a man whose soul's well-being was more important to him than his material wealth. Job called down the curse of heaven upon him if he had lived in selfish luxury: "If I have denied the desires of the poor or . . . if I have kept my bread to myself, not sharing it with the fatherless . . ." (Job 31:16,17).

Wealth is neither a sin nor a gift to be avoided.

The key factor is our *use* or *attitude* to it. So often people will declare that "money is *the* root of all evil," but that is, of course, a misquotation of the apostle Paul's words. He declared that *"the love of money is a root of all kinds of evil"* (1 Tim. 6:10).

Wealth can be a tremendous snare to those who possess it. Amos had to pronounce God's judgment on the people of his day who allowed their material wealth to make them morally and spiritually complacent (Amos 6:1-6). In two of our Lord's parables He portrayed rich men who were spiritually foolish (Luke 12:13-21; 16:19-31). One of the saddest incidents in the Gospel narratives is the story of the rich young man who declined to take up the Lord Jesus' invitation to discipleship because he loved too much his great wealth (Matt. 19:16-26). But while snares are real, they can be avoided. If wealth were an impossible snare to avoid, God would not make some of His people wealthy. Yet He undoubtedly does do so. But their wealth is a privileged stewardship.

The problem so often is that wealth can be *hoarded* (Jas. 5:3). And it may be hoarded because it is loved, and loved so much that there is a reluctance to use it. Whereas the truth is that God gives wealth so that it may be used and employed for good purposes. For us today wealth tends to mean money in the bank and the material assets represented by bricks and mortar in a house. But in earlier times men's principal assets were grain, clothes and precious metals. The rich fool felt that he was well off because of the grain stored in his extended barns (Luke 12:18). When Gehazi, the unfaithful servant of Elisha, tried to benefit from Naaman's healing from leprosy, he asked Naaman for "two sets of clothing" (2 Kings 5:22). Our Lord Jesus told a parable of how a man found someone else's treasure in a field, treasure that someone had hoarded and hidden in the ground (Matt. 13:44).

Hoarded wealth has God's blight upon it, if He so chooses. The grain, apparently safely stored in the bigger and better barns, can rot (Jas. 5:2). The clothes carefully placed in the wardrobe can be eaten by moths (5:2). And gold and silver, hidden away— perhaps in the ground—can become tarnished (5:3). All the things that we may foolishly hoard are perishable, and are open to being spoiled and ruined in some way—in marked contrast to true spiritual wealth (see 1 Pet. 1:4). Even the seemingly most permanent things like silver and gold lose their external brightness if hoarded and are doomed ultimately to decay and dissolution. The powerful snare for all who are materially wealthy is that they may deceive themselves about the security of their possessions, foolishly imagining that their wealth and prosperity are permanent.

Hoarded wealth often has God's blight upon it for an obvious reason: hoarded wealth has not been needed by its owner, but it may have been needed to have been used for the benefit of others. The poor beggar named Lazarus longed "to eat what fell from the rich man's table" (Luke 16:21), but the rich man gave him little or no thought. Waste is abhorrent to God, whether it comes through hoarding or extravagance. As Calvin wrote, "God has not appointed gold for rust nor garments for moth; but on the contrary He has designed them as aids to human life." When food rots, clothes become moth-eaten, and hoarded money loses its value, it may sometimes be evidence of their misuse.

We may wonder at first why James is so forthright and forceful in his condemnation of hoarded or accumulated wealth. The explanation is found in verse 4: the desire for wealth may make an employer pay low wages. The employer may justify himself by declaring that times are hard and that he can't afford more. But none knows the truth about his finances better than God. Unfortunately, men may be content to live in luxury and self-indulgence when innocent and poor people are unfairly treated because they have no resources to fight back (Jas. 5:5). (One possible interpretation of "the day of slaughter" is that it is a period when the poor are ill-treated or "slaughtered" by injustices in the courts, while the rich are unconcerned and content themselves with the enjoyment of their hoarded wealth and sometimes ill-gotten gains.)

The desire for wealth may be so great that men may be prepared to condemn innocent men in order to lay their hands on it (5:6). They may use their influence to coerce or bribe judges to condemn innocent men. We would be blind to ignore the fact that wealth can lead to injustice because of the power that it brings (5:6). Many of the cruelties of society spring from greed and avarice, arising not from poverty but from the possession of money. The possession of money seldom leads to satisfaction but rather to the desire for more, and yet more, money. Coveting other people's possessions may even make people prepared to murder (5:6)—and the despicable action of Jezebel with regard to Naboth's vineyard illustrates that sad fact (1 Kings 21:1-29). Whether our wealth is large or small, we all need to recognize that God knows the truth about our wealth—how we acquired it, how we view it, and how we use it. In the final analysis we are accountable to Him.

The plain conclusion from James's warning about the abuse of wealth is that it is foolish to put too high a value on it because of the perils it brings. Time and time again we hear echoes of the Sermon on the Mount in James's words. "Do not store up for yourselves treasures on earth, where moth and rust destroy, and where thieves break in and steal," our Saviour urged (Matt. 6:19). Material wealth may spoil through keeping, and is always vulnerable to theft and destruction. Wealth in heaven, however, is not vulnerable to decay or theft. Our Saviour went on to say, "But store up for yourselves treasures in heaven, where moth and rust do not destroy, and where thieves do not break in and steal" (Matt. 6:20). There is nothing wrong with being wealthy. It may often be God's reward for diligence in our work. But the danger is that our wealth should be limited to this world.

Wages

A wage is a repayment for work done. The prophets, from Amos onwards, proclaimed loudly and clearly that God requires that men should be paid a fair wage. A fair wage is a fair recompense for the work done. The Old Testament Scriptures laid down definite principles about the payment of wages. The Lord said to His people through Moses, "Do not take advantage of a hired man who is poor and needy, whether he is a brother Israelite or an alien living in one of your towns. Pay him his wages each day before sunset, because he is poor and is counting on it. Otherwise he may cry to the Lord against you, and you will be guilty of sin" (Deut. 24:14,15). Similarly in Leviticus 19:13: "Do not defraud your neighbor or rob him. Do not hold back the wages of a hired man overnight." Jeremiah pronounced judgment on kings who were unjust employers: "Woe to him who builds his palace by unrighteousness, his upper rooms by injustice, making his countrymen work for nothing, not paying them for their labor" (22:13).

God is involved in men's daily employment, in labor negotiations and the wages and salaries that are paid. "He who oppresses the poor shows contempt for their Maker, but whoever is kind to the needy honors God" (Prov. 14:31). Unfair wages ring the alarm bells of heaven. "Look!" James exclaims, "The wages you failed to pay the workmen who mowed your fields are crying out against you. The cries of the harvesters have reached the ears of the Lord Almighty" (5:4). The cries of the unjustly paid reach God's ears. When no one else listens, He attends very carefully.

The consistent testimony of the Bible is that God always hears the cries of those who call to Him (Ps. 18:6; 34:15; 1 Pet. 3:12). But more than that: He is also the unnoticed Observer of our work. He is the unseen Checker of wages and salary scales. He knows the recompense that the employer can and ought to pay. To fail to pay proper wages amounts to theft on the part of an employer (5:4). Cain was told that his brother's blood, which Cain had spilt through murder, cried out to God from the ground (Gen. 4:10). And injustice of every sort cries out to God and is noted by Him, and this includes injustice on account of unfair wages.

Not a few of us may be involved at times in determining the wages of others. We may not be the actual employer, but we may have to make recommendations. We must handle such affairs justly, and we must act in the way we would expect others to act towards us. Workers must be prepared to work hard, and employers must be prepared to pay well. As it is sin for an employee to withhold proper diligence in his work, so it is sin for an employer to withhold proper wages. Those who pay wages or have any influence in their determination must remember the certainty of God's judgment. One of the main ploys of Satan is to make men and women dismiss the idea of judgment as fanciful. The first doctrine he ever denied was judgment (Gen. 3:1,4), and he persists. But judgment awaits him, and those who listen to him.

Judgment

The principal thrust of James's warning to rich oppressors is that there is to be a judgment. Those who abuse wealth are going to be punished at that judgment. Misery is going to come upon them (5:1). Being so sure of it, James bids them act now as they will then: "Now listen, you rich people, weep and wail because of the misery that is coming upon you" (5:1). The context shows that he is not writing to all who are rich, but to the rich who *abuse* their wealth.

The judgment will be a time of wretchedness, distress, trouble and misery. The misery will be so immense that men will be caused to weep and wail (5:1). Weeping and tears can be of anguish rather than repentance, particularly when repentance has been resisted. It will be too late for repentance then. The word *wail* carries its meaning in its sound. "Wail," urges Isaiah, in his prophecy against Babylon, "for the day of the Lord is near; it will come like destruction from the Almighty. Because of this, all hands will go limp, every man's heart will melt. Terror will seize them, pain and anguish will grip them, they will writhe like a woman in labor. They will look aghast at each other, their faces aflame" (13:6-8).

On the day of judgment the hoarded and corrupted wealth of those who have misused their affluence will testify against them (Jas. 5:3). Perhaps we have all had the experience at some time of getting caught—or of being in danger of getting caught at doing what we shouldn't—particularly when we misbehaved as young children. Perhaps we raided the larder and finished off the jam tarts, contrary to instructions, but forgot to wipe off the jam from around our lips! Our parents had no doubt of our guilt because of the convicting evidence on our faces. In an infinitely more serious way, on the day of judgment there will be no prospect of hiding the convicting evidence of the abuse of wealth. The "corrosion" that has corroded possessions will bring about the justified downfall of their owners.

It has been suggested that the idea in verse 3 is of

rust so corroding that it eats into human flesh, like the wearing into the flesh of a rusty iron chain—a dreadful picture of the disastrous results of regarding money as the principal support and aim of life. But the main point James makes is that on the day of judgment all the evidence will be there, nothing will be missed, and it will speak for itself. The rich who have been foolish in the handling of their wealth will realize their folly in hoarding up possessions "in the last days." They will know that the evidence proves that they have no excuses to offer. "The last days" is a common expression in the New Testament. The last days are sometimes thought of as beginning with the birth of our Saviour (Heb. 1:2) in that God's new and final order of things—through the redeeming work of His Son and the consequent birth of the church—came into operation. The last days also describe the period of history immediately preceding the second coming of our Lord Jesus Christ (2 Tim. 3:1), the great event which will mark the completion of the present age. Both meanings fit the context here.

We need to have a picture in our mind's eye of a wealthy person happily surveying his grain in his barns, examining his wardrobes full of clothes, and checking his carefully stored boxes of gold and silver, quite forgetful of the unfair wages he may have paid out, and the urgent needs of the hungry and the homeless around him. He may think that all he has accumulated is just splendid and wonderful. But, in fact, the stores of accumulated wealth he surveys will become in effect a store of divine wrath from which God will draw on the day of judgment. The challenging truth is that those who store up wealth that has been wrongfully acquired store up anger for themselves (Rom. 2:5). Unjust salaries and wages (Jas. 5:4), as well as all other injustices, will be recompensed on the day God has appointed.

The day of judgment will be "the day of slaughter"

(5:5). James writes of that day as something already present. He writes as the Old Testament prophets often spoke and wrote: God's judgment is so certain in the future that it can be spoken of in terms of the present. He uses an illustration from the prophets when he writes of "the day of slaughter" (Isa. 34:6; Ezek. 21:15). This picture puts the luxury and self-indulgence of the rich in a proper perspective. They are like sheep jumping about with excitement at the lush pastures into which they have been brought, not knowing that it is a preparation for their slaughter.

I live in the city of Edinburgh, and close to our home, just two or three minutes' walk away, there is a hill with a large field at its foot. Although in a city, the surprising thing is that the field is often full of sheep. It's a delightful picture to behold and makes the spectator feel that he is in the country rather than in the heart of a huge city. The grass is green and lush, and the sheep seem to have everything going for them. But the truth of the matter is that they are in rich pastures only temporarily. They have been brought up from the country in preparation for the market and the slaughterhouse. Tomorrow or the next day they will no longer be there; the day of slaughter will have come.

Unjust payers of wages, and people who are wrongfully wealthy, are like cattle happily feeding, feeling totally secure, unaware of the day of slaughter tomorrow. As the writer of Proverbs says, "A stingy man is eager to get rich and is unaware that poverty awaits him" (28:22). Richard Baxter, the godly Puritan pastor, complains in one of his writings that "rich men are not acquainted with the true use of riches, nor think of the account which they must make to God of all they have; they think that their riches are their own, and that they may use them as they please."

"The day of slaughter" (Jas. 5:5) will be the day on which the Son of Man, our Lord Jesus Christ, reveals Himself (Luke 17:30). "That day will bring about the destruction of the heavens by fire, and the elements will melt in the heat" (2 Pet. 3:12). Described as "the great and glorious day of the Lord" (Acts 2:20; Joel 3:14), Jesus Christ our Lord is to be Lord of this day (1 Cor. 5:5; 1 Thess. 5:2; 2 Thess. 2:2; 2 Pet. 3:10), and it will be the last day of this age (John 6:39,40,44,54; 11:24; 12:48).

Money may have enabled some people to avoid human judgment because as it is often said "money will buy almost anything." But money and possessions provide no immunity against "the day of slaughter." There is no avoiding it because it is "the Lord Almighty" (Jas. 5:4) who will execute it. Behind the title "the Lord Almighty" is the Hebrew word *Sabaoth* which is a military epithet of God: He is the Lord of hosts or the Lord of armies. It is employed to demonstrate that the Lord is the Saviour and Protector of His people at all times. All the heavenly powers—"the hosts"—are ready to obey His command to defend His people. It expresses the truth of God's omnipotence. The oppressed, therefore, have the Lord Omnipotent as their helper and avenger.

The story is told of a man being brought before an American judge, justly accused of a horrible crime. Through some legal technicality, the judge was obliged to discharge him. But as he did so, he chose to say what he thought of the matter. "I believe you guilty," he said, "and would wish to condemn you severely, but through a petty technicality I am obliged to discharge you. I know you are guilty, and so do you; and I wish you to remember that you will some day pass before a better and *a wiser Judge*, when you will be dealt with according to justice, and not according to law." However impossible the situation may appear to the unjustly treated, the last word is with God. One day *all* injustices will be put right. The day of judgment will be the day for the rectifying of the wrongs of this world.

We need to mark these things and to cause them to condition and influence our thinking and perspective. "Now listen," James urges (5:1). "Look," he exclaims (5:4). These are solemn things for us to keep in our memories—and not least the certainty of God's judgment. If James's readers lived in "the last days," how much more do we!

During the winter of 1722-23 Jonathan Edwards wrote the majority of his "Resolutions," a series of rules formed from the Scriptures to act as a constant guide by which he should try his heart and life. One of the final resolutions was, "Resolved, Never to do anything, which I should be afraid to do, if I expected it would not be above an hour before I should hear the last trump."

Since saving money has a place in our Christian duty of providing for our relatives, and especially our immediate family (see 2 Cor. 12:14; 1 Tim. 5:8) and it is not wrong to save and to be provident, what is the difference between proper and legitimate saving and the hoarding of money? When does the desire to save become the desire to hoard?

James 5:4 mentions the cries of workmen about injustice and the cries of unpaid harvesters reaching God's ears. What do these facts teach us about God's character?

The world may choose to ignore the truth of God's imminent judgment of the world by His Son. But as Christians we should make it part of the warp and woof of our thinking. What difference should the certainty of God's judgment have upon our thinking and our behavior?

Twelve

THE NEED FOR PATIENCE
James 5:7-12

In normal English usage the two words *patience* and *perseverance* are almost synonymous, and we may often use one in place of the other with little difference in meaning. The Greek equivalents, however, tend to be more precise in their meanings. James employs the word *patience* in chapter 5, verses 7, 8 and 10 and then *perseverance* in verse 11. We have noticed earlier that *perseverance* is really "stick-ability" at its best—the determination to see a thing through no matter how great the obstacles. *Patience*, however, denotes the prolonged restraint of anger or agitation. Whenever it is used, there is perhaps a hint of resignation, but at the same time an element of brave persistence. Patience sums up the attitude of the person who is willing to await events rather than trying to force them.

Patience is extolled in the book of Proverbs: "A man's wisdom gives him patience; it is to his glory to overlook an offense" (19:11). "A patient man has great understanding, but a quick-tempered man displays folly" (14:29). "Better a patient man than a warrior, a man who controls his temper than one who takes a city" (16:32). Perhaps the principal reason for the extolling of patience is the fact that it is a characteristic of God Himself, who is "slow to anger" (Num. 14:18; Ps. 86:15; 103:8; Nah. 1:3). This ability to put a rightful brake upon the expression of anger is exactly the quality James longs to see reproduced in his readers by God's Spirit.

James has been dealing with the subject of injustice (5:1-6). Injustice is extremely difficult to bear. It is a most severe form of suffering. The more undeserved it is, the more natural it is to be angry. Injustice can lead to depression because of the feeling that nothing can be done and that all is lost. On the other hand, it can lead to revolution and violence. For God's people, however, it is meant to lead to patience.

James's words apply to all forms of suffering that may come to God's people. He does not have only the suffering of injustice in mind—such as the failure of employers to pay just wages—but also the suffering of persecution (5:10) and that which both illness and disaster bring (5:11). There is, of course, a very close link between patience and perseverance. When injustice and suffering occur it is important not to become angry with an anger that gets out of control—that's exactly where *patience* comes in. At the same time it is important to be asking, "What does God want to bring out of this situation for my own spiritual good and for His glory?" We then seek wisdom to see the situation through unflinchingly—and that's where *perseverance* comes in.

The Proper Focus of Patience

Patience, quite simply, means being prepared to wait (Jas. 5:7a). It involves being ready to wait for God to act and intervene with His own unique vindication. It is not, therefore, the mindless, disillusioned waiting of unexpectant people which can, unfortunately, mark many groups of unjustly treated people throughout the world, who have given up hope of ever being vindicated. The Christian's patience has a specific focus: "Be patient, then, brothers, *until the Lord's coming*" (5:7). The Christian's "blessed hope" is the glorious appearing of our great God and Saviour, Jesus Christ" (Titus 2:13). When the Bible uses the word *hope* it does not mean that of which we are uncertain—as does our contemporary use of the word—but that of which we are absolutely certain but which we have not yet experienced.

As believers in our Lord Jesus Christ, we have a glorious assurance for the future. His second coming will be in marked contrast to His first. He will come in clouds with power and great glory (Matt. 24:30; 26:64; Rev. 1:7)—the glory of His Father (Matt. 16:27). He will come with His angels (Matt. 16:27; 25:31; Mark 8:38; 2 Thess. 1:7), and with all His saints, in flaming fire (1 Thess. 3:13; 2 Thess. 1:7). It is much easier to be patient when you know that there is a fixed future point when the need for patience will be removed because all injustices will be dealt with—and that fixed point is the certain return of our Saviour (Phil. 3:20,21; Acts 1:9,11).

Two thousand Lisu Christians (refugees from China) gathered some years ago at Christmastime for a three-day conference in North Burma. It was noticed that passages about the second coming of our Lord Jesus Christ were underlined in blue and red in the dirty and thumbstained New Testaments of the refugees. Their questions were almost 100 percent concerned with the glorious hope. The assurance of our Lord's return is intended to color our whole perspective on life. But we need patience. Second Peter 3 discusses the apparent "delay" in the Lord's return. It is not a matter of a definite post-

ponement. Rather it is because of God's patience—
the same word for the patience required from us—to
give men full opportunity to repent (2 Pet. 3:9).

A Model of Patience

James employs an illustration with which all his
first-century readers would have been familiar—that
of a farmer (5:7b). "Farmer" may be an almost too
sophisticated description in that the word implies
simply someone who tills the soil. While there is
much hard work required of the farmer, there is one
thing he has to learn to do well, and it is to *wait!*
First, he must wait "for the land to yield its valuable
crop." He knows that what he waits for is valuable—
even as we do as we wait for the Lord's coming. He
knows that it is worth waiting for with patience. Secondly, he waits "for the fall and spring rains." The fall
rain is in late October and early November. Without
it, the seed which the farmer had sown would not
germinate. The spring rain, in April and May, was
essential if the grain was to mature. Much as the
farmer anticipated his valuable harvest, and much as
he had to play his part in the operation, the primary
requirement was patience.

God has His own times and seasons with regard to
our Saviour's return. When the disciples tried to
elicit greater detail from our Lord, He replied, "It is
not for you to know the times or dates the Father has
set by his own authority" (Acts 1:8). He immediately
then proceeded to commission them to be His wit-
nesses—in other words, to be like farmers who carried on with their work in anticipation of the great
harvest day.

Our Lord Jesus Christ Himself anticipates that
glorious harvest (Isa. 53:11), and we shall share in
His joy on that day. But, meanwhile, we must wait
and work with the quiet and expectant patience of
the farmer.

Patience's Good Companion

There is such a thing, sadly, as a miserable patience. Perhaps in our mind's eye we can see a person persevering under difficulties, but all he or she says and does seems to be aimed at eliciting sympathy: "Do look at me! Aren't I unfortunate? I need your pity!" Such people are sorry for themselves and they expect everyone else to be sorry for them too. But this is not a picture of *Christian* patience in the face of difficulty.

James repeats once more the proper focus of Christian patience and endurance—the Lord's coming—and reminds us that "it is near" (5:8). The assurance of the Lord's near return makes all the more important patience's good companion—*standing firm*. "You too," James urges, "be patient and *stand firm*, because the Lord's coming is near." Literally, "stand firm" is "establish your hearts." The verb carries the thought of fixing something firmly, or making something secure. Its use here by James implies that when we exercise the kind of patience he encourages, we shall fix our hearts very deliberately upon the Lord's coming which will give us stability in the face of all the hard knocks meted out to us. We have every reason to be stable because our confidence rests upon the unchanging God (Jas. 1:17) who has given us His unchanging word (1 Pet. 1:23) that "He who is coming will come and will not delay" (Heb. 10:37).

Patience and Restraint

Christian patience puts a restraint upon our grumbling against each other. Grumbling is a common human feeling. It is never more prevalent than when things are difficult in some way or other. Grumbling is a way of releasing some of our bad feelings. People may even argue that they feel better after a good grumble!

But, as we have seen earlier when dealing with slander (Jas. 4:11,12), grumbling is a form of judging. When we grumble, we are declaring that someone has either not done something that he ought to have done, or that he has done something wrong. When we grumble, therefore, we judge.

If, however, we exercise patience and develop Christian stability—with our eyes on the Lord's return—we appreciate that His return will herald the Day of Judgment. We must, therefore, leave all judgment to Him. And He is well-equipped to judge, and He's ready to judge—in fact, He's "standing at the door!" Sometimes God the Father is spoken of as the Judge (Heb. 12:23), and sometimes the Lord Jesus Christ is (Acts 10:42; 2 Tim. 4:1,8), as here. The two truths are brought together in the fact that God the Father has fixed a day on which He will judge the whole world in justice by our Lord Jesus Christ, the Judge whom He has appointed (Acts 17:31). Part of the Father's honoring of the Son is His appointment as the Judge of all men and women.

Few take grumbling seriously. But God *does* take it seriously. And so does every Christian whose focus is on the Lord's coming. The manner in which we judge others in our grumbles against them is the way we shall find ourselves judged (Matt. 7:1,2).

The Prophets' Example

So often when we suffer we imagine that we are unique. But, of course, that is not the case. Examples frequently help, and especially if they are of those whom we would naturally admire. James quotes, therefore, the example of "the prophets who spoke in the name of the Lord" (5:10). He has to describe them in this way because there were also false prophets, and they, significantly, escaped much of the suffering that the true prophets knew.

There was no doubt that "the prophets who spoke in the name of the Lord" were in God's will. They were commissioned by God and were doing His work; nevertheless they suffered persecution and extreme hardship. Elijah was hounded and hated (1 Kings 18:10,17). Jeremiah was thrown into a cistern with the threat of starving to death (Jer. 38:1-13). Amos was falsely accused of raising a conspiracy and was told to go back to where he had come from (Amos 7:10-13). Once more we have James reflecting the Sermon on the Mount in what he says. Our Saviour declared, "Blessed are you when people insult you, persecute you and falsely say all kinds of evil against you because of me. Rejoice and be glad, because great is your reward in heaven, for in the same way they persecuted the prophets who were before you" (Matt. 5:11,12). Stephen challenged his persecutors by asking, "Was there ever a prophet your fathers did not persecute? They even killed those who predicted the coming of the Righteous One" (Acts 7:52).

The prophets were not without their battles—for they were human like ourselves; but they learned to accept their sufferings with patience. They persevered in doing God's will in spite of the opposition. They fixed their eyes on what God had promised, and in particular upon "the coming of the Righteous One" (Acts 7:52). We, therefore, have even more reason to be patient and to persevere than they did. We live in the enjoyment of that to which they looked forward. Our Lord's second coming gives our patience an added focus and encouragement. We must fix our hearts firmly on it.

The Ultimate Blessing of Perseverance

James switches now from "patience" to "perseverance" (5:11). It is obvious that both virtues do not depend upon quick returns. Perseverance, like patience, implies waiting, and a *sustained* waiting of the "returns" or promised benefits are not quick in coming.

But a general principle of the Christian life—uniformly set forth in the Bible—is that God's blessing ultimately rests upon those who *persist* in doing the right thing. This has been the main thrust of James's teaching about the importance of perseverance when the Christian faces trials. If persistence is persisted in, the tested Christian becomes "mature and complete, not lacking anything" (1:4). What we know as "the Beatitudes" of the Sermon on the Mount all describe *sustained* attitudes. A beatitude is a supreme happiness, and James employs the same word *blessed* as our Lord does in the Beatitudes. The blessedness promised in each Beatitude is not necessarily a happiness experienced in the present moment or the immediate future but a happiness promised later, as the result of sustaining a God-pleasing attitude. For example, in the continuation of the eighth beatitude, which is directly relevant to James 5:10, the promised blessing is a blessing in the life after this. "Blessed are you when people insult you," said the Lord Jesus, "and falsely say all kinds of evil against you because of me. Rejoice and be glad, because great is your reward in heaven, for in the same way they persecuted the prophets who were before you" (Matt. 5:11,12). Perseverance may well be rewarded in this life, and it usually is. But it will be *completely* rewarded in the life to come.

A great proof of the blessing of perseverance is the record of Job's life, and of one thing there is no doubt—Job suffered. He suffered *materially* when all his worldly possessions were taken from him—his oxen, donkeys, sheep and camels (Job 1:14,16,17). He suffered *emotionally* when his sons and daughters were killed as the result of a hurricane and the collapse of the house in which they were feasting (Job 1:18,19). He suffered *physically* as he was covered with painful sores from the soles of his feet to the top of his head (Job 2:7). He suffered *mentally* as his wife encouraged him to abandon his faith in God (Job 2:9), and as his friends in turn showered upon him their conflicting advice.

But Job persevered. In spite of all that the devil, the enemy of our souls, threw at him, Job trusted God: "Though he slay me, yet will I hope in him" (13:15). In the heat of the spiritual furnace in which he found himself, Job exclaimed, "I know that my Redeemer lives, and that in the end he will stand upon the earth. And after my skin has been destroyed, yet in my flesh I will see God; I myself will see him with my own eyes—I, and not another. How my heart yearns within me!" (19:25-27).

Job's perseverance was the consequence of his faith. His faith *worked!* His perseverance was itself a work of faith. Although Job had to exercise patience over a long period, his perseverance brought the precise blessing which James argues is always God's pattern: "You have heard of Job's perseverance and have seen what the Lord finally brought about." The book of Job ends with the remarkable testimony that "the Lord blessed the latter part of Job's life more than his first" (42:12). What is more, Job's character was improved to his lasting good. He lost nothing of his character in the furnace except his unworthy characteristics. As Job himself declared when the heat of the furnace was on, "But he knows the way that I take; when he has tested me, I will come forth as gold" (Job 23:10; see also James 1:4; 1 Pet. 1:7).

Job's perseverance and the blessing it so obviously brought to him proved that "the Lord is full of compassion and mercy." As the psalmist declares, "Great are the works of the Lord; they are pondered by all who delight in them. Glorious and majestic are his deeds, and his righteousness endures forever. He has caused his wonders to be remembered; the Lord is gracious and compassionate" (Ps. 111:2-4). God is not simply compassionate, but He is *rich* in compassion. He is not only merciful but He is the God of *great* mercy (Ps. 25:6; 40:11). The Saviour who came "full of grace and truth" (John 1:14) was the perfect revelation of the Father, the visible image of the invisible God (John 1:18; Col. 1:15).

We ought never to forget, too, that the greatest example of patience and perseverance in the face of suffering was our Lord Jesus Christ. "For the joy set before him [he] endured the cross, scorning its shame" (Heb. 12:2). And His patient perseverance was wonderfully rewarded: He is "sat down at the right hand of the throne of God" (Heb. 12:2). It was appropriate that the writer of Hebrews should then write, "Consider him who endured such opposition from sinful men, so that you will not grow weary and lose heart" (Heb. 12:3). We may have to wait a long time sometimes in order to see God's final purpose, but while waiting we may be sure that "Behind a frowning providence, He hides a smiling face" (William Cowper).

Patience's Controlled Speech

James won't allow us to escape the implications of genuine Christian living upon the use of our tongue (5:12). When we are under pressure, especially if unjustly treated, the tendency is to speak with greater emphasis, and sometimes with exaggeration, more than we might do at other times. And it is most likely for this reason that James deals with the subject of swearing—of using oaths in daily conversation.

The original purpose of an oath lay in guaranteeing a man's word. A higher court of appeal was frequently provided by calling upon God. The formula of oaths originally had the character of conditionally cursing oneself if the statement should prove to be false. But, unfortunately, this could lead to using God's name, in order to add emphasis, in the swearing of an oath.

The fact that James introduces this section with the words "above all" implies the importance of the restraint we ought to exercise in this matter of swearing and oath-taking. These words constitute James's final quotation from the Sermon on the Mount when our Lord said, "Again, you have heard that it was said to the people long ago, 'Do not break your oath, but keep the oaths you have made to the Lord.' But I tell you, Do not swear at all: either by heaven, for it is God's throne; or by the earth, for it is his footstool; or by Jerusalem, for it is the city of the Great King. And do not swear by your head, for you cannot even make one hair white or black. Simply let your 'Yes' be 'Yes,' and your 'No,' 'No'; anything beyond this comes from the evil one" (Matt. 5:33-37). Our Lord attacked the Jewish custom of oath-taking in which the attempt was made to avoid the misuse of God's name. And this explains the references to swearing by heaven, the earth, Jerusalem or even one's own head.

Our Lord urged absolute truthfulness in every word we speak. Our "Yes" is to mean "Yes," and our "No" is to mean "No." It is sadly possible to be so expert in *using* words that at the end the hearer is either uncertain or no clearer as to what we really feel and mean. Unconditional truthfulness must be the pattern of the Christian's speech.

In the context, however, of suffering—whether of injustice or persecution or some other pressure—we must particularly watch our speech. Pressure so often means that there is an explosion—an explosion of speech and of unnecessary words. When the going is difficult, we must be all the more careful to aim at sincerity and simplicity of speech, avoiding all exaggeration. A life which exhibits the fruit of the Spirit—part of which is patience (Gal. 5:22)—will include self-control, an aspect of which is control over our tongue when under pressure.

The Lord's coming is an encouragement to patience. Concerning what sort of matters is it an encouragement to be patient?

Grumbling is really a form of judging one another. Does it find a place in our lives? Is it a matter of temperament or is it a bad habit we may acquire if we are not careful?

Words are an invaluable means of communication. In what unfortunate ways may words be used so that they cease to be a means of communication?

Thirteen

FAITH AT WORK
James 5:13-20

This final section of James's letter deals with three main subjects. It seems at first the most difficult part of the letter for which to give a title. But when we remember that James's major theme has been the relationship between faith and works, the title "Faith at Work" exactly fits because all three subjects are concerned with the putting of our faith to work in most practical and down-to-earth ways.

Daily Human Experiences

Faith must be put to work in all life's ups and downs (Jas. 5:13-16a). Four human experiences are mentioned in which we may all find ourselves sharing any day: trouble, happiness, illness and sin. *Trouble* (5:13) represents any circumstance or trial which brings into our life either suffering or the potential for misery. Paul used the same word for his "suffering" when he was treated like a criminal and chained in prison (2 Tim. 2:9). "Trials of many kinds" (Jas. 1:2) are the norm of the Christian's life as of the

person who is not a Christian. They are varied, and
many-colored. And yet at the same time, daily life
may equally well provide its *happiness* (5:13). Just as
the weather may one day be dull and miserable and
then the next bright and sunny, so life may be a mixture of troubles and joys. Often it is the troubles
which help us appreciate the joys.

Illness (5:14) is a trial against which we are given
no immunity as Christians. We have no power over it,
and there will be occasions when we are completely
weak and powerless because of disease or ailment.
Healing is often God's will but not always.

Sin (5:15), sadly, is also a factor in our lives. Our
new birth (1:18) brings about an entirely new attitude to sin so that we hate it and cease to sin in a
habitual manner. But we do not cease sinning. In
fact, the more we grow as Christians and appreciate
the glory of God's holiness, the more we become
aware of our sin.

We all share these four human experiences. While
we live in the world we cannot escape them. Implicit
in what James says, there are important priorities if
we are to cope with them.

The first priority is prayer (5:13). When trouble
comes, our first—and not our second or third—priority must be to pray. Many of us find it easy to run to
other people or to feel terribly sorry for ourselves
when difficulty arises. But as children of a wonderful
heavenly Father, our privilege, through the merits of
the sacrifice of "our glorious Lord Jesus Christ" (2:1),
is to have immediate access into the presence of God,
where "we may receive mercy and find grace to help
us in our time of need" (Heb. 4:16). We are encouraged to bring every trouble to God (Phil. 4:6,7; 1 Pet.
5:7).

The second priority is praise, and praise in song
(Jas. 5:13). We are created to praise, and we have
been redeemed by God so that we may declare His

praises before men (1 Pet. 2:9; Rom. 15:9). James does not suggest a brake should be put upon cheerfulness. Rather the best possible outlet for our happiness is praising God because "every good and perfect gift is from above" (Jas. 1:17). As we praise God for a particular source of happiness, it is not long before we remember His greatest gift and see all His other gifts in perspective. By praising God in this way, we help others besides ourselves; and we may well assist our brother who is in trouble, for by our song of praise we may turn his thoughts to the Lord. Christians have always been renowned for their singing. When Pliny, the Roman governor of Bithynia, wrote in A.D. 111 to Trojan, the Roman emperor, to tell him of the Christians in his province, he stated that his information was "that they were in the habit of meeting on a certain fixed day before it was light, when they sang in alternate verses a hymn to Christ as God."

The third priority is an established church relationship (Jas. 5:14). The Christian who is sick is instructed to call "the elders of the church to pray over him and anoint him with oil in the name of the Lord" (5:14). We know from the Acts of the Apostles that Paul and Barnabas, for example, "appointed elders . . . in each church" (Acts 14:23) which was brought into being by their missionary endeavors. James takes it for granted that his readers will recognize the place of the local church and its leadership. The New Testament as a whole always assumes that Christians living in the same locality will have regular fellowship, meeting together as a company of believers (1 Cor. 1:2; 14:23; 2 Cor. 1:1; 1 Tim. 3:15). The instinctive act of Paul, after his conversion, was to identify himself with the church at Damascus, and then with the believers at Jerusalem on his arrival there (Acts 9:19,26). Christians are assumed to be in such a close relationship together that they acknowledge certain men as spiritual leaders (Heb. 13:7)—as "elders" (Jas. 5:14)—and that they are glad to have the relationship. It is so often in the rough and tumble of human experiences that we prove the wonderful blessing God gives by means of the fellowship of His people in the local church.

The fourth priority is the confession of our sins (Jas. 15b,16a). The confession of our sins is a condition of walking in fellowship with God and with our fellow-Christians (1 John 1:6-9). Our primary confession must be to God Himself, of course, for He alone can forgive our sins (1 John 1:9). But often our sins have involved other people, and the honest confession of our sins to God demands the putting right of wrongs, and even where that is impossible, confessing our faults to others so that our relationship with them will be right, even as we want it to be also with God.

One of the particular snares into which Satan, our great enemy, would lead us is imbalance or going to extremes. Some have wrongly interpreted this exhortation to mutual confession as meaning that we should confess *all* our sins to one another, and James does not say this nor is it suggested elsewhere in Scripture. Hearing of other people's sins may be most unhelpful to us (see Gal. 6:1b). Confession of sins to one another should be engaged in only where it is both necessary and helpful. If I have wronged someone by my actions or my words, it may well be right that having confessed my sin to God, I go then and confess my sin to the person concerned. It may not be at all helpful, however, if I do the same with regard to the thoughts I have had about someone. To confess sinful thoughts to God is always right, but not to one another.

Another snare is that some have read into James's words the implication that illness is always due to sin. But that is a misreading. James says, "*If* he has sinned, he will be forgiven" (5:15). It is obvious that sin, especially sin that involves the misuse of our bodies, may bring illness. Paul implies, for example, that some of the Corinthians were "weak and sick" and a number had even died as part of God's judgment upon their sin (1 Cor. 11:30). But nowhere is it suggested that illness is to be immediately associated with sin—that is a mistake (John 9:1-3), and it is a suggestion that Satan often makes to disturb sensitive men and women. The apostle Paul himself suffered illness, and it was not a judgment of God upon him (2 Cor. 12:7-10).

What is obviously true is that when we are ill we usually find time on our hands to think. Such opportunity will be profitably used in self-examination—although we must avoid introspection—and it is appropriate that we should examine our relationship to God. That examination may lead to confession of sin—and it invariably does. There will be occasions when it will be tremendously helpful to share with a close Christian friend God's dealings with us.

The fifth priority is corporate prayer (Jas. 5:16). When we genuinely share with one another—and not least about our weaknesses—the most natural consequence is to pray together, and for one another, that our experience of God's forgiveness may be real and that we may be strengthened to withstand temptation. The healing that James mentions may be either on the physical level or on the spiritual. Peter uses the same word when, speaking of our Saviour's death, he writes, "By his wounds you have been *healed*" (1 Pet. 2:24). As we pray for one another, and as we pray together, God may graciously grant physical restoration to those who are ill. When physical healing is not His will, we may be sure that it is always right to pray for inner and spiritual healing where that is also the individual's need. When all is well within, the individual is strong to face all that is going on in the physical realm. Though outwardly we may be wasting away, we may be renewed inwardly day by day, as our relationship with God is right (2 Cor. 4:16).

A Problem

James 5:14-16 touches upon the subject of healing, and we must not pretend that the topic does not present problems, especially when those whom we love suffer. What we may say, in brief, is that God *can* and *does* heal in answer to prayer, and especially as we follow the procedure James lays down.

We must also say that it is not always God's intention to heal. What James says here must be looked at together with the other Scriptures dealing with illness and healing (see Gal. 4:13,14; Phil. 2:27; 2 Tim. 4:20.) The apostle Paul's own experience was that it was not God's will to heal him of his illness, but instead to give him grace to bear it so that his dependence might be greater upon the Lord Jesus Christ (2 Cor. 12:7-10). And we probably all know godly men and women, whose faith and characters are an example, who suffer physical disability and illness.

Certain important principles are established here regarding anointing and prayer for healing. *First, the initiative is to rest with the person who is unwell.* "Is any one of you sick? *He* should call the elders of the church" (5:14). The elders are not to suggest to the unwell person that he should ask for it. The individual who is unwell may not feel that it is appropriate—and his conviction is respected. On the other hand, God is able to lay it upon a person's heart that this course of action is right for him.

Second, the elders—or the spiritual leaders of the local church—have a special responsibility to respond to this request. They are under shepherds and men of Christian maturity and discernment. It is not for the members of the church to do this for one another—it is the responsibility of the spiritual over-seer.

Third, we are not to imagine that there is any-thing "magical" about the anointing with oil. Although medicinal properties were attributed to olive oil, these are not emphasized. Rather, impor-tance is attached to the prayer that accompanies the anointing. Our Lord Jesus did not need to touch the leper or the blind man's eyes as he healed them, but there was undoubted value in these actions for the two persons concerned, and similarly with the anointing with oil "in the name of the Lord." That the anointing is "in the name of the Lord" is the factor that is significant, perhaps symbolizing God's protec-tion and blessing upon the individual, a particular encouragement if he is under attack by the enemy of souls.

Fourth, it is likely that in his reference to "the prayer offered in faith" (5:15) James refers to the special gift of faith. Literally, his words are "the prayer of faith." All true prayer involves faith (Heb. 11:6), and James must have in mind the gift of faith the Spirit gives (1 Cor. 12:9). As the elders gather around the person who is unwell, having anointed him with oil in the name of the Lord, the Lord may give them special discernment to know exactly how to pray. Sometimes it may be that they should pray for grace to submit to God's will in the suffering (2 Cor. 12:9). But on other occasions the Lord may give the enlightenment and confidence to ask for very specific healing and it will be granted.

Fifth, there is special benefit for the unwell per-son in this spiritual exercise even if physical heal-ing proves not to be God's will. When we are unwell, it is extremely difficult to pray for ourselves with objectivity because we naturally want to be restored to health. Our spiritual under shepherds are in a much better position to pray for us with discernment. In addition, when we are unwell we may find it almost impossible to pray at all. And here others may help us. As the elders pray with him, the sufferer is able to rest in the knowledge that through corporate prayer his circumstances are placed under God's control afresh, and that if physical healing is not God's will, he may be sure of the spiritual healing he needs and the daily renewal of God's grace and peace.

Trouble, happiness, illness and sin—none of us knows when we may have to face these ordinary, everyday human experiences. But when we do, our faith must be put to work whether in prayer, praise, fellowship, confession of sin or corporate prayer.

The Practice of Prayer

Faith must be put to work in the proper employment of God's gift of prayer. James reminds us of a basic principle of which faith needs to lay hold: "The prayer of a righteous man is powerful and effective" (Jas. 5:16b).

First, we must make sure we understand what James means by a righteous man. A righteous man, first and foremost, is a man who is in a right relationship with God. A righteous man, therefore, is a reconciled man who has entered into the benefits of justification by faith. But, as James has been at pains to point out, faith is seen in what a person does (2:24). Hence a righteous man is a reconciled man who is striving to live rightly (see Jas. 1:20; Matt. 3:15). He knows, for example, that if he cherishes sin in his heart, the Lord does not listen to him (Ps. 66:18), and he, therefore, strives to avoid all known sin.

A reconciled man who lives rightly—"a righteous man"—may be expected to be a man who prays. Prayer will be the strength or mainstay of his life. It will be the secret of his God-given influence in the lives of others. It will be the secret of his influence because of the power of such prayer. It is "powerful and effective." Prayer is competent to cope with all difficulties; it is able to do things when every other means of changing a situation has failed.

To illustrate the truth of this principle, James chooses the example of Elijah. In case we immediately put aside his example because he was such an outstanding servant of God, James reminds us, "Elijah was a man just like us" (5:17). Whenever we hear of an outstanding believer, we easily feel ourselves outclassed. We think, "I could never match up to his standard." Elijah had all the frailty of human nature, even as we do. Frailty, weakness—in fact, our humanity—is no obstacle to effective prayer. Prayer is God's chosen benefit for weak and frail human beings.

Five things are told us about Elijah's praying (5:17,18). *First, Elijah prayed earnestly.* Literally, James writes, "in prayer he prayed." Or, he prayed in his prayers. Elijah's prayers were not just words or a formality. He meant every word that he uttered. It is possible for us to use a lot of words when we are supposedly praying, but for those words to be only words and not true prayer at all.

Second, Elijah prayed specifically. Initially he prayed that it might not rain, and then after three-and-a-half years he prayed that it might rain again. He did not pray in generalities, but for specifics.

Third, Elijah prayed believingly. His earnestness and specific requests were part of his faith. In fact he staked his life on the certainty of what he asked God to do. He stood before Ahab and declared in the light of his prayer, "As the Lord, the God of Israel, lives, whom I serve, there will be neither dew nor rain in the next few years except at my word" (1 Kings 17:1). And those significant years later he told Ahab, "Go, eat and drink, for there is the sound of a heavy rain" (1 Kings 18:41), and he went to the top of Carmel and prayed for the rain to come (1 Kings 18:42-44).

Fourth, Elijah prayed in accordance with his understanding of God's will. The two requests James mentions were obviously Elijah's understanding of God's will. In fact, the historian records that "the word of the Lord came to Elijah" (1 Kings 17:2). When we pray in the will of God our prayers are always certain of His answer. To pray in the will of God and to pray in line with our understanding of God's Word are virtually synonymous. The Scriptures are given to us so that our prayers may be guided into God's will.

Fifth, Elijah prayed with God's honor in view. We find Elijah praying on Mount Carmel, "O Lord, God of Abraham, Isaac and Israel, let it be known today that you are God in Israel and that I am your servant and have done all these things at your command. Answer me, O Lord, answer me, so that these people will know that you, O Lord, are God, and that you are turning their hearts back again" (1 Kings 18:36,37). Elijah longed for the people to acknowledge God as they ought. God answered Elijah's prayers, as he put his faith to work in his prayers. Prayer honors God, and God honors those who pray.

Spiritual Wanderers

Faith must be put to work in the restoration of spiritual wanderers. Spiritual wandering is a sad feature of Christian experience, and in James 4:1-10 we have already considered backsliding and the way we are to return to God when this happens. If we ask, "Who are these spiritual wanderers that James has in view?" one relevant answer is that they are those who have separated obedience from faith, obeying from hearing. A couple of important clues are provided as to the identity of those James has in mind. First, the verb "to wander" is also capable of being translated "to be deceived" (see 1:16). Second, the word "error" (5:20) is the noun from the same verb.

Satan himself is the great deceiver (2 Cor. 11:14), and he employs false teachers and others to try to mislead God's people and lead them astray (Matt. 24:4-25; 1 John 3:7).

"The truth" (Jas. 5:19) is "the truth that is in Jesus" (Eph. 4:21), which is contained in "the word of truth" (Jas. 1:18) by which we have received the gift of new birth as we have trusted in the Lord Jesus Christ for salvation. James's rightful and sustained emphasis has been that the truth demands obedience as the proof of our new birth. To wander from the truth, therefore, is to live in a way that contradicts the truth, that fails to show the relationship between faith and works, that means that our lives are no more productive of righteousness than the demons who profess to believe (Jas. 2:19). Whenever we wander spiritually, like lost sheep, we have always lost sight of the truth and of Him who is the Truth, our Lord Jesus Christ.

Whenever a true believer wanders, however, there will always be someone—and usually more than one—who feels concern for him. God ensures that is the case because He is the Shepherd (Ps. 23:1), and His Son is "the Chief Shepherd" (1 Pet. 5:4). His loving concern expresses itself through the concern He puts into the hearts of His children for those who are wandering. They will want to see the wanderer brought back, and they will go after him and not cease praying and working until he is "back" with them again in the fellowship of God's people.

Such a restoring work saves the erring individual from death. To live one's life in a state of separation from God is spiritual death, and to remain always in that state is to be doomed to live in eternal separation from Him. The restored wanderer is delivered from the first plight and has assurance that he will be delivered from the second as he lives in obedience to the truth of the gospel.

Such a restoring work also covers over "a multitude of sins" (Jas. 5:20). In view of Peter's similar use of this phrase (1 Pet. 4:8), it is probably right to assume that this was a popular expression in the early church, having its origins in Proverbs 10:12: "Love covers over all wrongs." The question may be in our minds as to whose sins are in view—the wanderer's or those of the one who seeks after him? Nowhere is it ever suggested that we can earn the forgiveness of our sins, and so we must reject the latter suggestion. Rather we must understand James as saying that love covers up a multitude of sins in others by the forgiveness it shows and generates. When we really care about the wanderer or backslider, we long to show him the grace and kindness God has shown to us. God does not remember our sins any more and we strive to do the same with regard to one another's sins.

We are to be in no doubt about the value of this restoring work—"remember this," James urges (5:20). And it is a work that is usually successful. We should not fail to notice that James actually addresses the potential wanderer or the returned wanderer in verse 19. When God is behind our seeking after the restoration of those who are wandering, He may be counted upon to assist us in the completion of the task.

If perhaps we wonder about the connection between verses 19 and 20 and the immediately preceding verses, the answer is probably that nothing is more important in the restoration of a spiritual wanderer than prayer. As one goes out to seek him, other Christians join together in prayer that the seeker may have success.

Is our church fellowship one in which it is easy to share our troubles and happinesses and the spiritual burdens that we bear? What can we do as individuals to increase the warmth and reality of our Christian fellowship?

What illustrations can you provide of the power and effectiveness of prayer, first, from the Bible, and second, from your own and other people's experience?

It is plainly right that we should be concerned for the restoration of those who have wandered from the truth. How will we know if we are the ones to go out after them? And what qualities are required of us if we are to be effective in doing so? (It will be helpful to look up verses like 1 Corinthians 10:12 and Galatians 6:1.)

Other Studies From Regal's Popular Bible Commentary For Laymen Series